The World Within

Dr. Delbert Blair

Inner Alchemy's Publishing

Chicago, IL

Second Edition

978-0-9961266-7-0

Any trade names, trademarks, service marks, etc. mentioned in this publication are for identification only. Therefore, any specific company or product mentioned is owned by their respective owner and not by Inner Alchemy's Publishing. Further, the company or product mentioned neither owns, endorses, nor has heard of Inner Alchemy's Publishing. By stating this, we can avoid printing the ®, ™, ©, etc. marks that we might otherwise have to place throughout the text.

The publisher does not participate in, endorse, or have any authority or responsibility concerning private business transactions between our authors and the public.

Published by

    Inner Alchemy's Publishing (Inner Alchemy's)

    332 S. Michigan Ave.

    Ste 1032-C141

    Chicago, IL 60604-4434

    info@inneralchemys.com

    www.inneralchemys.com

Printed in the United States of America

Dedicated to a friend, who was also like a son to me since we became acquainted and who has helped me and heard my inner thoughts and comforted me in my times of need and without his help this would have never came to exist. Thank you Tony

To the extra-terrestrials I met so many years ago who've showed me there is more to this universe, earth, and more importantly showed me the true strength that lies within me.

This work is a direct transcription of the lectures that took place in 1998.

CONTENTS

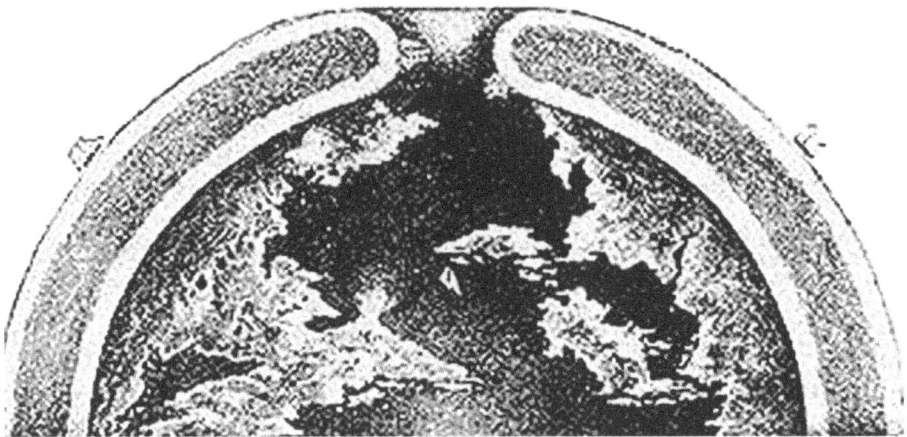

The World Within
Part 1-1

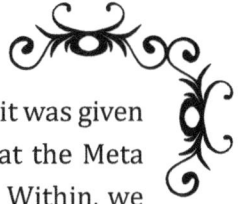

*T*he name of the lecture is the World Within and it was given by Dr. Delbert Blair on February 28 of 1998 at the Meta Center in Chicago, IL. The lecture the World Within, we will take a look at the deep study of our planet earth. We will also take a big jump and begin to look inside our earth and see if there is an analysis for many of the things that have happened currently that have happened in the past that we can begin to make sense out of some things tha normally have been glossed over. Most of us are hearing about spaceships and weather changes and surgical things that are now going on, implants, gene structure, gene manipulation. We are living in a time where the truth is either coming back or fiction should replace truth, because what we are hearing now seems almost incredibleto be true. What you are going to hear today might take that same leap with you, but most of you I feel in this sophisticated audience because you are into metaphysics, you are not new at, will probably take it with a grain of salt and do your own research and might even verify and substantiate some research you have already done yourself.

To do so though I want to look at some basic concepts that we have about our earth and to see if they all hold up. Were told in general that our earth of course has a top, a bottom, and an equator that were finding out now is perfectly spheroid or perfectly round like a ball that is somewhat elongated or bulging more like a doughnut. They say that the armature of the equator is 7927 miles, the polar axis and that's the idea that the earth is kind of shifted to the side and not straight up and down, where its top and bottom should be,or where north and south pole should be is 4900 miles at the area of the top and the bottom. The circumference round the earth itself is 24,960 miles. The latitudnal lines those that run horizontally if you would are what they set up to gauge what is and where is something on the globe itself. If you have a plane or you are driving it would show your latitude and your longitude lines of course or the points that run vertically. So if you are looking at al map, you use this more or less to tell you where you were

using fictional lines, and of course are as our political boundaries. If we looked at our planet without the political boundaries and like this, we would find very interesting things. The earth is said to be 595 billion tons. Im not exactly sure where they highly arrived at that conclusion, but that's the point of area that their giving and the weight again. The total surface area of the earth is said to be 196 million 950 thousand square miles.

The land surface said to 57 000 510 square miles and the water surface area again is said to be 166 000 square miles. The pressure to the cubic foot and this always amazes me because I guess we really don't feel that pressure is said to be 344.7 pounds to the cubic foot.So I guess we have some pretty strong exoskeletons or endoskeletons whichever you might state. The greatest height on our planet is supposedly Mount Everest and the Himilayas at 29,028 feet. The greates depth the Phillipine Trench in the Pacific Ocean, some 37,982 feet. The earth is also said to have a molten interior with a crust again resting over this molten exterior and what they call Plato's ship or continental displacement. It was said that even though the interior is molten, the land area builds up to where the water is and many continents that extend around it more or less float on what they call plate tectocplates. Im sure you heard about it on the Ted Cauber or somebody, what is it Ted Copell, where he said that there was a blue pyramid but it really was an illusion cause it was formed by two tektite plates rising up and forming a bridge. Well understand that our continent is said to be on a tektite plate and if it rolls up I think either one or the other of the shores would be in bad shape. But nevertheless this is what their saying. The earth is said to be 5 to 6 ½ billion years old, that means that there is a billion and a half years difference. And you think a billion and a half years might be a long time.So when you say 5 to 6 ½ billion years that's really precise. I would think just a billion and a half years off.

And life on earth being some 2 billions of years old and that is said to be chemical life, intelligent and biological. With man is said to

be only some 8000 years old and some religious groups say its 6200 years old because they say that the Garden of Eden and the first man was created 4004 B.C. All of these things are probably no more true or no more false than what we are going to soon hear tonight. But I live to tell you some of the things that we take as statistically correct may not exactly be. And last of all the distance of our earth to the sun is 93 million miles. Our sun is only 93 million miles away. Now they state again that our earth again has a molten interior, that it has an inner core, an outer core, a mantle, and then a shell. The dimensions of the shell are said to be some 30 miles thick, made out of granet base salt and of course some sand and loam if you would. That the mantle itself is said to be some 1800 miles thick.The outer core some 1360 miles thick. The inner core some 1630 miles thick. And that intrests me too the 30 miles tag on both of those. And the molten center can reach temperatures of up to 8000 farenheight.

This is why again to live in the center of the earth, iit would be possible you would burn up, because it is a molten sea with this buring molten lava or whichever else it is. Yet with all of these statistics and all of the travel, and topography and so that our scientists are able to give, our earth is still a very mysterious place. And many things happen upon it that seemingly don't get into the classrooms don't make the radio until of course recently with the art bell show and all. And things that are going on a regular basis that either defy description or either causes people to look for another analogy in order to reach the conclusion as to what is happening. This is a model earth globe you see here. For those of you that are buying the tape or happen to come to some of our lecture.

And this globe has no unnatural boundaries, there are no political breaks in it, there is nothing on it to let you know whether its Russia, China, or japan, whether it's the United States orAfrica or Europe it just shows our globe as it would be if it were twirling in space again. Now what you will notice on thisglobe as we look at it, is that it has a lot con-volutions and corrugations. It is not smooth. If you notice in the water ar-

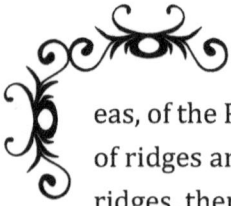

eas, of the Pacific and the waters areas of the Atlantic, that there are a lot of ridges and crescents there are what they call estuaries, what they call ridges, there are valleys, there are mountains, and there are fiords. And all of these are to let you know that this planet has undergone a lot of change. Now when you take away the unnatural topographical changes and so, you will see that there are mountain ranges here vs. all the way to Alaska, all the way down to west coast, all the way down to South America, all the way down to Argentina, almost all the way down to South America or what they call again Antarctica.

A huge mountain range ok. If you notice again, in the pacific, there are a lot of convolutions especially off of New Guinea, off of Japan, Reortee Island. All kinds of things under the water, which you normally can't see. There are ridges, there are estuaries, there are mountains, there are valleys, everything that is there. And if we spin around to the Atlantic area, between Africa and our East coast if you would you'll notice something there that is very very interesting. You'll notice again what is called the mid- Atlantic ridge and it runs also past the San Adreas fault line. The San Andreas Fault line is in the pacific, but the mid Atlantic ridge you will see is a long ridge that goes right down and it's in the middle of the Atlantic Ocean. That is a huge ridge. It means its like a mountain and a valley that has been carved out of the bottom of the Atlantic ocean there and it is a fracture that is in our planet, where something has where something has rendered, whether it was a huge ocean quake, whether something open and closed there. Its hard to know, but the ridge is still there. Its called the mi– atlantic ridge.

The intresting thing is that when you also look around, you will find some of these mountains that break the surface of the ocean. That's when they are kind of colored green or round if you would. Now youll notice where they break the surface of the ocean, these are just mountain ranges which we now call islands. But, we are seeing the tops of these islands if you would. The Azor islands are one of those things that go along what we call our central ridge. They have found writings on many of these

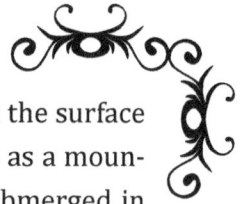

mountains in many of these caves whether they are beneath the surface of the ocean or whether they pierce the ocean and come up as a mountain range. Writings, now if the writing is on something submerged in the sea it means that either somebody had to put on diving gear and hold their breath and began to carve on mountains now beneath the sea or at one time those mountains were probably above sea level. Now if you find these things in the middle of the pacific or the atlantic ocean, it begans to shed some light. I would think so. There are two kinds of writings that the anthropologists, the archaeologists, and generally topogrophists of our earth or scientists say there is what they call hieroglyphs and something called pertoglyphs.

Hieroglyphs is gotten from the Greek word Hyros which means sacred and glyph of course means writing ,carving something along this line. So a hieroglyph is said to be sacred writing. Im not sure what sacred writing means, but that's what the term hieroglyph comes from. Petroglph is from the Greek word petro meaning rock. And of course we use petroleum, which is shaved shell rock that is compressed to get oil and gas. And this is of course writing. So petroglyph again means again writing on rock, not on papyrus or ancient so called text, but again on these kinds of things. Glyphs are not only found under the water, but they always seem to follow streams that come from the big body of water as those writing for there and somebody riding came upward or the streams are bigger than they are now have now been reduced to streams.

Whichever way you would, they are found in Ireland, they are found in Spain, they are found in north Africa, they are found in the Canary islands, they are found in the virgin islands, they are found in the yucatan peninsula,they are found in along the gulf of Mexico, they are found along the mississppi river, the Rio grande and the Colorado, and they are found in the gulf of California in the baja Penninsula, they are found in Utah, they are found in Arizona, in Hawaii, Asia, Babylon, Egypt, china, japan, wherever you go you can find either pertroglyphs or what we call hieroglyphs. In the Grand Canyon, they have found on the sides of the mountain glyps. And most recently, and let me say also that there are some so called Indian tribes that we refer to them as first worlders or the original Americans, the ancient name for them was glautamans and algonquins, and one of the most ancient names you can find is incadians, the correct pronunciation for the people that they are. There have been many of them know that have been going back to the bottom of the Colorado Rocky Rivers, because in the Grand Canyon they now find streams that are drying up. The river that used to flow through the bottom of the Grand Canyon is beginning to disperse, its beginning to break up and many caves that were hidden beneath this water level are now becoming open. It is a place now where many strange things are happening, including anomalies seen at night, including energy of rays coming up out of the Grand Canyon itself. It can be seen in the night sky and a lot of activities happening now in the grand canyon of our own world. What I am simply saying to you that even though we have come a long way with our science and in America were said to have one of the best educational systems around, there is still a lot to learn and a lot of it is not being shared on a regular basis to the people. Because of that we are going to take a look, not to challenge anything that is being said, but to possibly add to. Because we feel that a lot of scientists and topographists already know what you are going to learn tonight. But they are not releasing it to the public in general.

The earth has many different things, but in the beginning to do study they find the zoologist and the biologists refer to animal life and how far and frequent that animal life can be and they date it and we then have a term called biological life. There are very interesting creatures on our earth. The camel, which is said to be yet a very African fauna, yet the fossils show remains of the camel can not only be found in Africa but in india, in South America, and in our own state of Kansas, which one of the members mentioned that they had recently went to. They have found fossils remains of the camel, yet they say it originates only in Africa. What was it doing over here? And if the fossil remains start

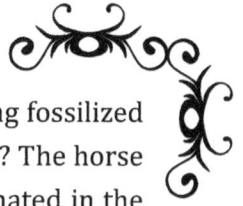

showing more than two or three thousand years ago as being fossilized how did they get here and why is it only in one state Kansas? The horse which everybody takes for granted again said to have originated in the western hemisphere yet fossilized remains of the horse can be found in fossil beds in Nebraska, in the bare tar pits, and in asia, and throughout Europe.

This is the same type of a horse that we see now. Cattle and sheep were said to be domesticated only and can't live without living in herds now a days and yet sheep and so were found in Europe, carvings of sheep were found in the caves throughout Europe in the Stone Age and huge buffalo herds that now roam America were said to have roamed South Central Asia. Buffalo herds have now said to have only originated in the Americas. The cave lion is said to be found in the Southwest of America can also be found in Europe. That we found again no way that these so called matings of this animal can take place agains whole huge bodies of water.

Were going to begin to look at some of the flora again if you would, there is the banana which everybody takes for granted is found in Mexico, Brazil, the Guan Islands, in Florida, and most of Central America, including the West Indies. Yet it is a native of said to be tropical Asia and tropical Africa. The banana is generally seedless and cannot be reproduced by cuttings and it has no tuber or root other than that which is on the tree but not on the fruit itself. Which means again how do you do something like that, how do the seeds spread, unless your leading to cultivation, unless someone takes it, plants it someplace else other than where it is indigenously found. They have found bananas supposedly covered with ice which means that it pre dated the ice age. And at this time America was not supposed to be tropical. How is it there? Why is it there? Everybody takes wheat for granted, for example everybody has wheat cakes and wheat bread and so on things like this, wheat have never existed in a seemingly wild state nor is there any evidence to trace its descent. But what is called previous fossil species. Wheat is found in Europe in five different varieties. Somebody had to work with that wheat

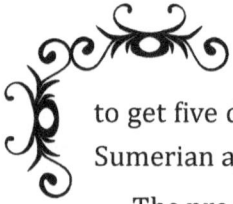

to get five different varieties of it. It has been cultivated during the pre-Sumerian age and if you read in some of the Zacharia Sitchen books.

The pre Sumerian age means in Mesopotamia. Mesopotamia 1 where they had wheat and during this time of course you had what was called an ice age. How could wheat have existed during this particular time and in five different kinds of grains if you would? This is though again as somebody had made these grains up, five different varieties, and placed them in various areas in our planet at least that is one way of looking at it. We have what is called a mixture of languages on our planet and because of this, it is very hard unless you do a lot of study to be able to communicate with each other because everyone speaks a different language. We find now of course now there is a school of linguisitics where people are beginning to learn or can have people know one langauge and act as interpreters. The phonecians which we get the word phonics and the phonetic alphabet along with the people called the Carthaginians again used signs for sounds. The type of language used presently in the Eastern hemisphere and for the first time according to modern anthropologists again it was used in the Americas of no more than about 100 or 150 years ago, someplace inbetween there. Yet, there are many types of languages that are found to overlap.

For instance if you can speak native Hawaiian, and very few people can and you can speak Gaelic or german bog youll find that you can undestand the same similar language. In fact there was a big fight that took place that's prior to World War II, when a group of German scientists home based again in Hawaii, and a group of Hawians were in a bar. And the German soldiers took and said an off color joke about a Hawiain woman. And the Hawian guy jumped over and started a fist fight and there was a big brawl that took place. And when they questioned as to what happened, he says well what did this guy say to you? He said well he didn't say anything to them, we were talking amongst ourselves. But they understood enough of what these German soldiers who were speaking more or less Gaelic to know that it was an offensive joke, yet

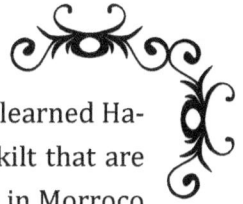

they had never learned German and the Germans had never learned Hawain. There is a lot of similiarities, even in dress with the kilt that are worn by the so called Irish and Scottish that are found again in Morroco and parts of Jamiaca and many places like this. And there is a very same thing called a kin whale, which the woman again in the islands and the women in parts of Africa would go at the death of a person.

They would set up a loud whale or moaning if you would and it was idea to honor the dead soul that this moaning or whale would continue. And it was supposed to last for three days and no one is supposed to break it or the spirit would be in unrest. Which meant if one woman, it is only by the woman, men were not allowed to do this, if one woman gave up the whale another was supposed to take this up.The same practice was done in Ireland. Its called a kin whale. The kining and quickening of the spirit whale. Yet, none of these people knew each other and where these practices come. Im going to cut through a lot of other substantiative things to let you see why I have reached a possible conclusion on this, to get to the meat of tonight's subject. But I will simply say if you do a little research you will find that there are many anomalies, many strange things about our planet, about the people of the planet, and about the alphabet and language of the planet that makes it very interesting. Ill stop with this one.

Many of us now, are having a migration or an immigration of people that are coming out of Latin America. They are coming out of Argentina, they are coming out of Mexico, they are coming out of Brazil, and theyre coming to California, theyre coming to the East Coast, they are coming all over the United States. The strange thing is things you will see now you will begin to see the native or this mestizo or nimbazi that comes out of South America. They look in many cases like Japense people. If you look carefully they have slant eyes, the same height, you will find again that their skin color is about the same and if you listen to them when they get excited, they began to huh nu hu. It sounds just as though they could be native Japanese or even Chinese.

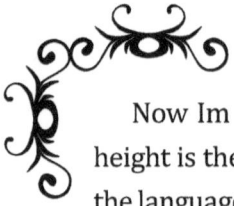

Now Im saying this to you because you can observe this yourself. The height is the same, the skin color is the same, and even when they talk fast the language begans to give an a tone, atonality that sounds the same too. Im suggesting that we many be closer to each other than we think. And if was not for something holistic that happened, we may all be one people. And the Christian bible refers to a time when the languages were confused and that the people were separated. And Im thinking some parts of that may be very true with a little research that goes along. When we also look at our earth we hear strange legends and strange stories. Stories of lost Atlantis. I guess everybody in here can give a dissertation for at least about five minutes about Atlantis, said to be a continent that was in the Atlantic Ocean somewhere. That's why it was called Atlantis. That this continent went down through a series of halocasusts and that the thing was pretty quick. It went down supposedly within a weeks time, some say within three days time. And therefore, the legend is supposed to be brought forth by Plato and Socrates, actually it was taken from Solan the Egyptian priest when the Greeks were in captivity before they came in from Alexandria and took over the area.

These were legends and stories that did not just start in Greece but were carried on by many people. There are legends about a continent that was in the Atlantic that was still held by the people in the Azors and many people on again the West Coast of Africa. There are all kinds of things about possibly Atlantis. Very little is heard, but some about the Lamooria, sometimes called a pawn or moo. And that in the Lamooria, which supposedly existed again in the Pacific Ocean, was a continent that was larger than any type of water we have now. That at one time our planet was manily land more than water, now its three quarters water. It's interesting if you look at the Pacific now you will find ridges, you will find islands, of course we know about the Haiwaian Islands, Gaunen, and Siapan. There are many places and many islands dotting throughout the Pacific, some of which are very interesting. If you take a look at Easter Island, some 1600 miles off the west coast of Chile, you will find again an island that has large statutes upon it.

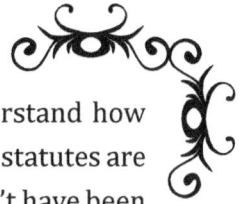

Statutes that are said to be monolith. Nobody can understand how they got there because there is no connecting land mass. The statutes are so strong and so hard in weight and tonnage that they couldn't have been taken over by any ship and yet they have found 22, 44, and what I understand now 100s because some of these have been buried over in topsoil just on the Easter Island area. And some of them are not made off of the indegenious base that you find on the island. The question becomes how did these statutes get there? If we began to think in terms of a possible land mass, continenet that was there and broke up, quarrying and stoning was going on and these are left isolated for the bigger land mass, it can began to make sense. If you also notice that one thing in common is held by most of the islanders when you start going back in their history.

They all look African or Negroid is a better way of looking at it now. There are many stories about Queen Kalahalni and Queen Kalahaluni and again the hawaian self which was ruled by a queen and later on a king in the figi, again to NewZealand, to any place you go, especially even to Australia a larger comtinent all of these people look very negrito. And that is a term that is used now by anthropologists, Negritos. That the indegenious people almost in any place on our earth if you go back far enough look Negrito. Small occipital lobe, their long headed, usually peppercorn or kinky hair, large lips or what they would call now Negroid types of features. This is one thing in common no matter where you go. Eventhough at the end of black history month, this is not where I just want to stop, but to let you know there is still a common thread wherever we go on our planet. It is just because of racism and so some of these things are not specifically taught. So im telling you its true and can be easily verified with a little research. But another thing also seems to come to the fore when they went to the North Pole and they talked to people that were migrating northward from Canada they called these people Eskimo and they ask the eskimo in general why do you migrate further north sometimes when the weather gets worse? And they asked them where do you come from?

The Eskimo seems to be a composite of almost every race that we see on our planet. And yet they are isolated until recently over the last sixty years from the rest of the people on our earth. The Eskimo does migrate north when the winters come and they have been found with their igloos and some of the tramplings pharaphanelia that they have far far up Bhafa Island, the area now which is known as the iceberg area. Which is a little snow crest as you can see again the little white line that goes around the top where there is a snow line certain latitude that they reach there. They asked them where did they come from. They said they came from the north. They said well of course you don't mean the north, because there is nothing up there but ice and snow. Where do you come from? And they say that their ancestors come from there. They also found that when they watched some of these tribes of eskimos they would leave with very little game, some of their dogs, a few other animals. Because of the harsh weather they didn't keep too many animals. But when they come back the next year they would have flowers, they would have seeds, they would have more animals.

The animals that obviously provigated. And they would ask them how do you this in the storm. And they say well we told you we came from the north. That up here in the north there is many wildlife, they had seeds and game and flowers. Well of course they were laughed at because everybody understands that is you go north past Canada youre not going to get seeds and grains, and flowers, and parats and cockatoos and other things like this. One of that began to rear its nasty head was during World War 11 and any of the pilots that tried to avoid radar and some of the gunners to reach Europe would go up near the poles and in many cases their planes crashed. And if they crashed, they were given provisions that would keep them alive for about seven day and usually a cyanide capsule because if their life began to get too hard to take. Now what they have found is that the down sailors and the down pilots, some of the shipwrecked pilots would say that they were plaugued by mesquito bites and sand storms. That the biggest thing that they had to worry about

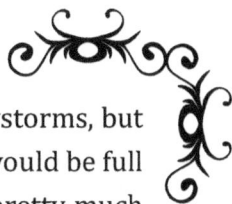

was not so much the further north they went with the snowstorms, but mequito bites and sandstorms and that the sky sometimes would be full of birds. All of this led to one conclusion later on which is pretty much reached by a statement made in 1956, by rare Admiral Richard Everlyn Bird. When Admiral Bird went to both the North Pole and later on to the South Pole, in 1956 he made a statement.

He said that this expedition has opened up a vast new territory and that this expedition will actually be the most important one that has ever been done on the planet earth that we know about. What he talked about as he went 2600 miles into the South Pole and 1600 miles into the North Pole when he flew in an airplane, not by dogsled in all of this, they actually flew planes. That the further north that they went the more that they found green vegetation, the more that they found what looks like the giant woolly mamooth, the more that they found flowers, the more that they found everything else. And the same happened when they went deep into the South Pole area. What they stated was and what they tried to hide was that our planet does not have poles. And I even found out, which you can do some checking yourself that there are no polar flights. Now there might be now with some of these supersonic airplanes around now doing mock 2 and mock 3.

But in most cases there were no polar flights. So flights would take off somewhere in the United States, would go up near the pole, but instead of going over the pole,they would go around the pole and then go to the area whether it was there or not. There are no polar flights. And one of the reasons ther are no polar flights, that the same type of thing is now occurring again on our polar earth, too many crashes. Now we are finding out that the planes are crashing cause the electricity does not work. They are finding out now that the transponders and when you are looking at the radar equipment no longer function. The gyro mechanisms do not function well and the people were following, the planes were following the curvature of the earth and the next thing you know they crashed to the ground. So the anomaly that is again let me say is beginning to happen as we speak now. What they have found is that the earth was not as we have been taught, that there are no north poles and south poles, that all of the things that were always in dispute when the British explorer, I forget his name right now all the way to admiral perry and all like this that they did not get to the north pole. And there is a lot of debate about both of those things.

That's why they have asterics by their names about discovering the north pole. Methaphysics states and research states that there are no poles on our earth. The area that is supposed to be a pole is a huge opening. That that opening is at both ends of our planet. And that opeining leads into what we now to what we call the inner world. That there is a portion of our planet that we have not been told about that can be accessed either through the north or South Pole and there are areas which we will get to see that connected that we shall see are also very interesting. Found that there was a satellite that was placed up in orbit that was called the essa, essa 3 and essa 7, this is sometime ago in the mid 50s and this photograph that you are going to see is one made by the essa 7 when a cloud covering was that generally was over the north pole was moved aside and what was able to be seen was a distinct hole leading into the interior. This is something that is very hard to get. They say it was never published. But I give you a picture of the supposed essa photograph which shows distinctly an opening there at the poles. The same thing was repeated at the north and south poles, the same kind of opening was seen into the earth. The conjecture had been and we will get more into that as we proceed in the series of the inner world that many planets may possess the same thing. And the idea is that if one planet is hollow and our moon is solid, then we have a phenomenon that cannot exist. If ever we prove that our earth is open and hollow, then the moon must be hollow or it would crash into each other because a solid and a hollow cannot stay side by side in a very balanced order.

If it is postulation holds it sets up a whole new concept about our science. And this is why this is one of the reasons, not the only one, you will

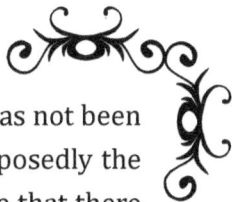

find that there will be many reasons why this kind of thing has not been revealed. This is again essa3 and essa7s photograph of supposedly the openings to the poles. Ancient ones have said for a long time that there have been people that lived inside the earth. If we here about orbiss's adventure to the undeworld, if we hear about amenta and the land of stix which there were said to be rivers and people that were believed in by the Egyptians and the Nubian people. Heres another cross section in general of the whole philosophy, with the dimensions being given of the innerside and ofcourse the innersum again.

There have been numbers of books that have referred to this concept and of course whether or not we believe it is a matter of opinion. But there is a book put out by Marshall Gardner along about the 1890s or so called the journey to the earth's interior. There was another book put out not too long ago by a man Emerson put out in the 50s called the smoky God referring to what was said to be the inner sun or proton's sun in the center of the earth ourself. There is another one which received a lot of acclaim, which you probably heard about the hollow earth by Dr. George Benard who also went to talk about Admiral Bird and Admiral Perry's events and what was said to be found there and the things that didn't seem to hold up about vegetation and fossil remains.

There is one that hardly anyone has heard about called the Shaver Mystery. It was a book written by Richard Shaver. This came out in the early fourties and it has been one of the most hidden set of books, becasuse it was almost eight of them. Many people don't even know that they have existed. Recently again there was the holy tabernacle scrolls by Dr. York and also the earth chronicles by zacharia sitchen. Which all refer to the possibility of there being other life forms inside the earth. Many of the so called hippies in the early sixties and to the early seventies again talked about what they called Alexander tokens middle earth by which a lot of trolls and little pollutions and so lived and it was said that they were visited and that many of the people that came out of the Caucasiod mountains that were people who used to live in middle earth. And that

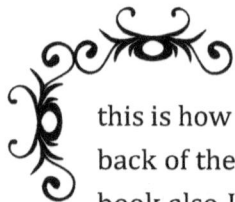

this is how this whole thing got started when they found drawings in the back of these caves there that seemed to refer to another land. This is a book also I have one of the original versions of the Hollow Earth by Dr. Geroge Bernard.

This is also one of the books that are hard to find. Having had the pleasure and privelage of meeting Dr. York, I aslo have one of his scrolls that talked about this. And of course we sold for a long time one of Zacharia Sitchen's books. Of course I say these are not the only things, cause you can find all throughout the bible, you can find in the el Koran, you can find in the popula, you can find the status of diezen, also find references to inner world inner life nand the fact that the surface people have never been the intelligent ones, they were always guided by the Gods that were in the earth. You have even heard references to the the Gods and Giants that were in the earth. Of course now we laugh at these things. Maybe I feel in the next seven months the laughter will stop because I make a statement automatically. Many of the UFOs that we think come from outer space come from our own planet. As races of people when calamities come have, have gone to hide inside the earth itself. That one of the biggest battles being fought now is for possession for some of the biggest cities by which there is air conditioning, by which there is pollution vaporizer, by which there is wonderful mechanisms and the battle is still being fought 30 miles down. Now when you bring out these kinds of things you began to step into deep waters and I think our planet is already in very deep waters as it goes.There is a hum that is being heard by many people. It has been referred to as a douse hum.

It is stated that this hum can be heard in valleys, can be heard in deserts, can be heard in cities at times, can be heard in rural areas when you get away from a lot of the city cacophony. And that this hum seems to come from everywhere and no where. They can hear it best near the ground. The douse hum is a drilling operation using what is called a mole, m –o – l – e. Molecular organizing laser equipment. A mole in which they actually had to construct a thing down in the earth itself. They took it

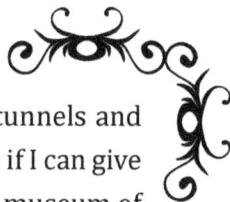

down at least three miles, and they found that there were tunnels and huge beds down there. And huge tunnels, some times as large if I can give an example here if we go right out here to 60th street by the museum of science and industry and run all the way down to 12th street, that's a tunnel. The height again can be anywhere from 800 to a 1000 feet high. These are tunnels not caves but tunnels that go throughout our planet from one part to the other.

These tunnels are also now being augmented. Don't let them fool you when they finally begin to rebuild it. They are not being built by this molecular organizing laser equipment or called mole they are simply being tunneled out further or using existing tunnels to make more. This activity is going on especially when Russia started to dig one of them to reach again by what they always talk about which is the bearing straights by which they stated many migration paths took place. I doubt that seriously. But they were digging an area to undergo Alaska going underneath the ocean there and this project has been called the globe project, it has many other projects too. There is of activity going on underneath the surface. I state that some of it is the United States government, some of it being done by the Russian government, although Russia is said not to exist as a state, and some of it is being done by people who they don't know who they are. And this activity that is happening beneath our surface of our planet on a regular basis.

And that hum is a drilling liquidizing machine that is exactly or was boring through some harsh areas. It is possible now to go from one continent to another without going in the air or taking a ship by going underground using the ancient tunnels and whole areas that are now considered to be caves.If we take the same scenario or concept and follow it again, the idea seems be that our earth not only has a hollow but it has a series of innerconnecting tunnels leading down to what is called the axel center of the earth itself.On the board im going to show you a large example of what were talking about. If the earth has an opening, that opening goes down to the north pole to the south pole and again exists at both the poles which

we are saying now that the point of this concept does not exist. That our earth actually breathes from north to south and that in the middle is the soul of earth what we call the proton sun giving off energy that is given through the north and south poles referred to as the aurora borealis.

That when you go far enough, you are trying to go over the poles, if you follow the land curvature you will wind up going inside and you will follow the land curvature until you exit the other side. But the only thing is that when you are doing that, you are going to see things that look a little differently and the sun will seem to change polarity and brightness, because when were looking at the huge sun rays outside, you will suddenly pick up what they call the smoking gun, a kind of smokycloud with clouds around it. There is a lot of moisture there. This sun looks different from the other sun which seems to be called the land of the midday sun or the noon day sun.

This is why if you go further north, north or south you will seem to go into a time where the sun has existed for almost nine months. In many cases if stay standing there or your moving to go to through the interior to exit at the other port. If you are living inside the curvature as some of these land masses do, then you will be seeing a different sun and if you back up a little bit you will begin to see the sun go away. What is called Mooie Malis and monoliths and so called saber toothed tigers and many things only exist inside the earth itself. And from time to time they are flash frozen by swimming in the waters from natural predators or none. They will get washed away into the North Pole area and then the water begans to freeze. One of the things that they found there is a checklist that icebergs are always composed of fresh water. One of the questions that has plagued scientists is how can icebergs be made of freshwater and found in saltwater oceans and encased in them sometimes a mammoth that is supposed to be ceased to exist a long time ago but they now have green vegetation in their mouth. And they say they must have been flash frozen which is proof of a galactic terminal or some type of a holocaust in which ice in a flash flood froze everything.

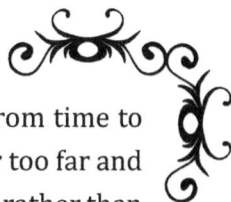

I state that is not the case, that they still exist and that from time to time they get on these little capes of ice because they wander too far and it breaks loose and as it gets into the colder area it exists here rather than at the poles because they are frozen and therefore they are now seemingly partly in tact, of course they died from suffocation, mostly green vegetation that they were eating that can be found inside the earth is still there. The second phenomena is that earth is said to be honeycombed with both mountains and mountain ranges, islands, and caves. If you're a speaologist or any type of a person who likes to go into caves you will understand that there are caves all over our planet. And the earth is said for this segment to be divided into six sections or six levels if you would getting down to hollow itself. Each of these levels affords more space when you take and combine then you would have total to live on the surface. Why? Because there is six levels with that same type of surface area. Each one becoming more conocentric as we come near the end. But in there are huge caves as big as cities and larger.

The connecting tunnels going to different levels, if you know where they are so that you could go exiting out into the earth for a long time. Your going to hear more and more about males holes all over the place. And now you can understand what males holes maybe. How many are familiar at all with the mell's whole phiolosophy. Just a few.

That is a person who supposed to live up in Oregon, again on the west coast in some of the areas that found a hole that people have been throwing frigidaires into, dumping dirt, and garbage into, even car parts into for the longest time and they never hit the bottom and the hole never filled up. We have called in again on the art bell show, now Im not acting as a proponent for it, but if you're looking for the way out stuff that is where you can hear it. Because one guy called up and told him about this. He likes to hear strange phenomena type things.

And he said well they have been doing this for a long time and recently though he began to get a foul smell that was coming out of there and also light rays seems to be coming out of there. So he called in because

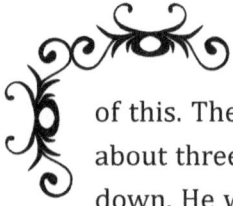

of this. The next day after he was on the show and he had him on for about three hours and he even made a song out of it called mell's hole-down. He was decked by mibs (men in black) and then later on by the United States government forces who rather because now he, you know they supposedly this show is listened to by 20 to 40 million people each night. Rather than just take him on out, they actually paid him to get off the land. First of all they told him he had to get off the land, that it was government property. What you understand about him and the domain is that none of us here own anything anyway.

It's just a matter of whatever situation that arises in by which they evoke imminent domain. But nevertheless they came took over his property and he was gone. The paid him a handsome amount and told him to keep his mouth shut till he was gone.These kind of stories about deep holes or these kinds of subjects or suddenly fractures appearing where vapor and sulfur come out that prolonged and existed for a long time. If you take this kind of a concept you can began to see that there can be many mels holes. And when you began to hear about the legends and creatures inside the earth, it doesn't necessarily mean that they are in the earth kind of hollow. That this is a pheneomena, it means that they can be living on any of these levels. Now two things stop you from believing that. We have been told that when you go into the earth it gets hotter and hotter.

That its molten lava. This is what volcanoes is all about. Understand that any mountain range you see was once a volcano. One of the biggest ones we have, what do you call it off the west coast, when you fly right over, the Rocky Mountains. That is this long range we showed you here. And when you look again at this you can see again it extends all the way up here at the Pole, all the way down, down. This was caused by a fracture. I make another Pacific smashing against the west coast of South America causing it again to rise up and you can see that that whole thing would happen there. If you check again how many of you have been out to the west coast or some time in the past. Just raise your hand. Ok. In-

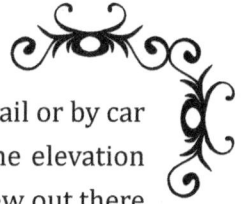

teresting thing, if you go out there, if you went out there by rail or by car you notice again you can cross the Rockies and you find the elevation going up and coming down. That's very interesting. If you flew out there you actually have to cross this huge desert area and then you have to get into until you see this mountain range. Once you cross of things change. Not only is the vibration out there different. They laugh about the west coasters. But the trees got bigger, they got more tropical, you got fruits and things. This is interesting if you are into produce and I know many of you are vegetarians in here. This produce used to come from California.

It was sweeter, bigger, and seemed to be more fulfilling; it had more nutrients, amino acids, vitamins, and everything else with it. Well that is because according to the metaphysical teachings and research because that was not part of alguanqa, which is the old name for what we know call now America. That that was part of Lamooria, the huge continenet that broke up here in the south pacific. Crashed against part of it causing this ridge after redrafted itself with the alguanquin continent. Therefore the United States is composed of many different types of things if you would, different not only as creatures but of land masses and the the Rocky Mountains west looks much different from the Rocky Mountains east. This is even with alhegainys. Things change there too. In the area we now call Pensylvania. In the area Ohio there is a peat moss fire that has never been put out. They can never be put out. They can't put it out. And this is why you will find most things over there very desolate. And except for the Blue Ridge Mountains and so in the black hills you will find that everything is very desolate. This is why you can get a lot of petroleum and oil fields there. But underneath is still a fire that they cannot put out. Because underneath the area of Pennsylvania, there is a whole tunnel or shall we say a whole continenet full of moss peat moss. And that peat moss is constantly burning that's why the area there is aways very warm and that's why when they began to drill oil wells in there they can hit the petroleum bed. Because they hit the petroleum bed there does not necessarily mean all around on that latitude on our planet there are petroleum fields.

Some of these cases along with this phiolosphy, there are whole areas of caves and even temperatures. Most temperatures at the caves is what 60 degrees, 60.7, something close. Meaning temperatures of the cave is the same. By the way it is now a felony, I don't remember when it went through Congress but somebody passed it, to go into a cave alone. Did you understand that? To be found in a cave now is a felony. Now I never knew that because when you go to mammoth caves or Lookout Mountain, you go to all these places, of course you go on these tours. But now somebody passed a law about going into caves. Its been stated that in Chicago right here alone underneath this very area there are landfills. If you remember about the World's Fair Exposition where they built the Museum of Science and Industry over there. That this area from at least the bedlake if you mess around going to Indiana all the way down to near Wisconsin in many cases its land fill. They want to get closer to the water area so they build a dam. The cave in many cases extended out to many places until halstead and in some places Ashland Ave.

Peninsulas in this area. What is also interesting about it, if you get one of the topographical maps, I don't know if you can still get it. This is one of the reasons that are around, that when they had the flood in Chicago they were very worried downtown, because there is a whole tunnel that leads all the way out underneath the lake. If you saw the movie relic, it even pointed that out to you. If you remember again when they had that flood they were worried about certain things happening because that water could have gone all the way over Ashland ave and in many cases made the ground there very saturated. With the floods were getting might be one of the excuses to hide that fact. This whole area has a huge underground tunnel area. Interseting enough as we speak about Chicago there are two churches, the one at 64th and Kenwood, the other there at Woodlawn at 63rd that actually have tunnel entrances that mesh with those tunnels down there. They have openings beneath and many things have said to be occurring strange in those two churches too. There are two different denoinations, but if you go by there you will still see them.

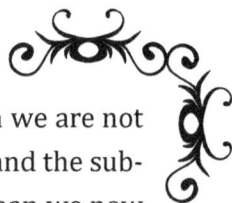

This is a strange area as we find most of our planet when we are not told about the subtaranean areas. The subtaranean tunnels and the subtaranean caves. Now we are going to take a huge leap. The leap we now take is if these places exist why is it that people don't live there. Or why is it again if they have this mean temperature and some way or another they can have air, someway or another things can, wildlife or life could be there. Why are they well known and why aren't they occupied. The story is that they are occupied. That there is a life form and that there has been life forms on our planet that we have not been told about and as we feel there have been ages that have came, when the dinosaurs left and so and the time for the wooly mamooth is gone, and the multie stusk elephant. That these creatures still do live there. Because its said that the center of our earth is a tropical paradise. It has had many names and there have been many legends. I am going to go over some of the names and legends and many of you will recognize them. Some of you may recognize all of them; some of you will recognize none of them, but ill go into it again. It's called the Greek Olympus, in nevadic its called mount neru or hemaldry, in scandanavia it's called the etus or esaur, egyptains reffered to the area as amentay, the city of seven petals the ishu, Ramans, and the Buddhists believe in, the city of the seven kings of Edith by some Chistrians and by some Jewish people, the Eden of the Hebrew and later Jewish people again was the same seven petals or the kings' kingdom.

The Tibetans know of Shamballa or the city sham of allah, the Persians alberti or ayana, the Hebrew cannon in the land of cannon, the Mexican tullah or the tollah nights, the Aztecs maya and mayapon, the Spanish el dorado the city of gold, the aboriginies monowah the place of monah that flew from the heavens, the Celtics duwat or denada, the chinyans or the Chinese the land of shivay or chinyah, the islands of Babylon and king Arthur and the british isles, the German whalah. And remember again I forget who it is Misorsky or somebody else was riding mahallah and so talked about the firebirds that went there. And so the firebirds the English utopia. There have been many names of course. There have been

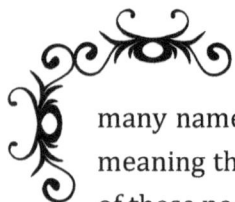

many names talking about shangrallah. Sha meaning earth and grallah meaning the hidden places. Shangrallah, paradise cocachehey, culky. All of these people are talking about a so called place where people live forever or their alive for a very long time, where there is milk and honey, where there is strange fruit, where the animals get along with the people and all these kind of things and of course they are reffered to as legends.

Let me state here now that one of the great secrets of the pyramids which we are about ready to be reveal because one of the earthquakes that hit already ruptured it. Is that beneath the great pyramid, there is another pyramid and that is found in the bottom of a huge cave by which people used to be able to run to the pyramid of the giza by following eight paths, eight tunnels leading to any part of the earth you wanted to go to. And when they had their meetings, the people would not travel to the surface. They would come up through these caves and some of the openings of course are still there. Another thing you must now understand is that the sphinx was built a long time before the pyramid and the sphix looked like a Negroid woman. As we will find that most planets have Negroid woman shinx. They found also that the pyramid was then built by those people who from altantis and the lost lamorians and again people from another planet who came here from another planet to share architecture to balance our earth itself. Now this sounds way out. The big thing that they had in common why it's hard to duplicate now is that they understood that the earth was hollow, they understood that gravity consisted of the push of this inner sun, the proton sun, and then vortex being set up by the outer sun. And once you used to tune into those vibrations you could travel with a whole new meaning to propulsion, you could levitate things, and people caught in that area began to quicken in spirit.

They began to be able to astral project, they began to be very psychic and many people could not take the vibrations. As it was said that the gift of the god would be given to them. The gift of the god we will find out was melanin. To move beyond as were going to do these things in series.

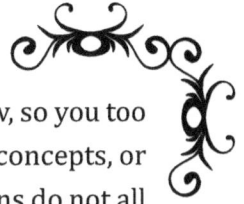

Were going to do everything that all these top scientists know, so you too have a chance to do whatever you wish to do with the ideas, concepts, or study. Many of the species of people that we now call earthians do not all orginate the same way. Ther are legends of people at the gates of nuerubaugh. If you hear about it, you can do some research called the green ones, in which it was said in the early, im sorry the late 1890s, near the turn of the century that there were two green people that appeared at the gates of nuremburg Germany. They were green. One was male and one was female. They were an anomaly and of course they were almost taken up as a side show except that they were well formed, shorter than a statue and of course the people there were very fair and the main of these people were green. It is called the story of the green ones.

It's easy enough to find. The reason why I bring that out is because one of them died. The boy died. The girl was able to eat the food that was here and lived. And as she ate the food and lived she turned pink and looked like any other German nuremburg citizen. The boy died because he could not adapt to that. The green coloring left him. And when they questioned the girl, when they taught her she learned to speak German and what she told them was that she came from a land inside, that there were many levels of this land, but she lived in the particular one where green vegetation was everwhere. That the light came from an unknown source but it seemed to emit from the caves and big openings in her cave central. They said stated again that these kids went on a little picnic and so they wandered away from the rest of the people, got lost in the tunnels, saw a great light, came up and found out that they hit the surface. As they had only heard legends of a surface and did not believe it.

She went on to talk about a lot of things and then suddenly one day after she had already amalgamated the soul, she went out into the forest and disappeared. They never understood what they called the story of the green ones. But if you find that, you will find that there are legends consisting of strange creatures all over our planet. If you go into South America near the Yucatan, in a place there you will hear the story of what

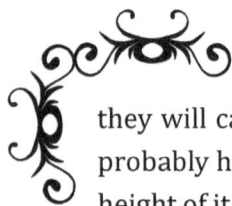

they will call the gill man. The gill man, there also is a gill woman. You probably heard about the creature from the black lagoon. Except for the height of it, supposedly there are in an area called lake poo poo. Now the Rocombo jungle areas and now where the rivers, lake poo poo is, this is where they have found little creatures that walk around that have gils and breathe but walk upright. They have webbed appendages. And from time to time have tried to mate or steal certain woman or surface woman if you would and amalgamation was seemingly successful in some cases. There is all stories about these little web creatures and they make a high grunting sound or im sorry a high pitched sound or a low grunting sound whichever again. But those stories exist everywhere. If you go into certain areas of Africa, you will find another strange tribe. The adambes which again they are people that look African, very tall, but their feet are closed claws. They have actually three toes with hooks on them, like a bird. Ah, there is stories, I think somebody brough a picture of that in to us, that was about three weeks ago of this strange tribe of people. There are always again anomalies that have been kind of shooshed off because there have been no one understood why they came about or where they came from. But you will also find that the great religions of earth all have one thing in common. They believe in a central figure. That central figure in many cases does not look like the other figures look, but everbody believs that they would come. And they usually have two supporters along with it. I give you this particular idea. In Greece there is multiplicities of what they call gods and golden ages. And these people usually come from indside the earth or downside from a great mountain. In Greece they have Uranus, Cronos, and Zues who supposeldy came to the people and had to even higher priestheads to tell them what to do. On India there is a story of dayas, dayas, kendar, and valunda. Again a trinity of people who supposedly came from the sky or either mountain tops and raised the consciousness of the people. In Isreal they have god, yaweh, and yahova. And supposedly you could not even say. And that is supposed to be yaweh or the teconometra. Yaweh, I don't know why you cant say it. Because as a person with melonin Im allowed to say whatever

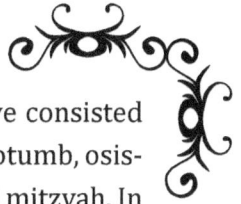

I want in this particular planet. But again these legends have consisted with it and it comes back and forth again. In Egypt they have otumb, osisrus, and Horace. The trinity again. In IIran, they had vaya, and mitzvah. In phonetcia, they had god, el, and bahel. The Hitiks had anu, kamarbe, and tasurbe. The Mexicans had amalato, pleccado and crisispecado. One thing they had in common was that they were all darkskin. Some of them blueblack, some of them with scales, some of them with tails. But all of them had great powers and they came to bring certain religions to all of these people. Even in the story of the laws of hamarabe, which is said some of the finest laws and some of the finest consciousness was brought to people from a mound in Babylon by Shamas who gave the laws to Hamarabe who brought them to his people. All of us are pretty much familiar with the Jehovah and Moses and the Ten Commandments came dowm from Mount Sinai. Another one you hear about is Zues who gave the creaton laws to minus on mount Ida.All of these mountains where these people go up and suddenly come back, siddenly they are transfixed. They began to transpose the consciousness of the people. And of course this is believed in by many of the people who are mohomidians again. That the arc angel Gabriel showed muhhamad a golden tablet that deals with mecca. All of these things are showing that something happened from time to time where people are transfigured by going to a mountain where they see a great light that does not go out and then they are changed. What was very much hidden and is beginning to be revealed now was for almost four years during the 1970s. And were not talking about 1870 on up down in Mexico City and down in many areas of Guatemala a huge light came over the city and for almost three years off and on people were being beamed up and beamed down. A whole group of people were transposed, transfixed, or something done to. The press refused to cover it and they only had some leakings coming out. I have some of thos clippings that happened down there in New Mexico City and many of the little jungle outclaves. If you go down there if you go to South America they have highways now saying you are now going into UFO territory. If you remember just the other day they had a huge UFO

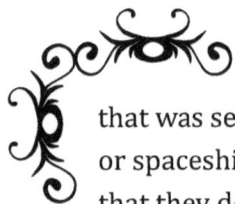

that was seen over Mexico City. People always seeing these little saucers or spaceships coming and going. And the Aztecs, Mayans, and the people that they do not refer to the Olmecs all had pictures of these golden tablets, supposed to be the sun discs, the sun gods, the people that came with this. And they wore headdresses and many of them looked serepentine like. And they still had the same type of headdresses with the same type of a serpent like nose now if you would and the petals or leaves or whatever you want to call it, the headdress going back. If you notice some of the stances of the mestizos and the adambeses people that are in South America the dances still show some kind of a god that looks like serpent and the big golden plate or the disc that was supposed to be where they came from. The flat what they call ziggeraut there shows a top that is flat and as you see the other pyramid was a equilateral triangle. The ziggeraut supposedly could land on the top and those openings were door ways where people could come out of the bottom of this craft, walk down and be honored and everywhere that you find that type of ziggeraut you will find serpentine figures, figures of snakes, or the upright walking serpents which had many names. One of the types of races that supposedly lives inside the earth is a serpentine race. But their said not to be indigenious to the earth itself, but to simply use as their ancestors did certain tunnels and certain cities by which ther are told that those people they help create and their own could be taken from time to time to be questioned and so on. This is their right. Down also you will find in certain areas there people that look somewhat Nordic, only much taller. The golden plumb lines if yo would. You would find also that the Negritos are people that look olmecian and if you're not sure about the Olmecs go back and does some black history study about how the Olmecs look. And in many cases when you are hearing about mayans and Aztecs especially the ancient Aztecs and the mayans, they are really olmecian people who had an understanding that came to this planet from another place and understood again their own. Earth people on the surface are an experiment. Earth people on the surface are already a mixture of many things. But the one thing that they gave to the true surface

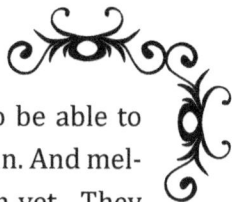

man was the ability when the golden age would resume, to be able to exist and live through it. They gave the gift of the gods melanin. And melanin is an adaptagin. That is why they cannot break it down yet. They don't know how to make it. They don't know how to reproduce it. They can only utilize it in its form and help to enhance it. It was a gift given to those prototypes put on the surface to be able to go anywhere on the planet, to be able to communicate telepathically with their creators and be able again to adapt to whatever happened. Other surface people it was reported again in grafted mixtures and they are doing the same thing again. Because the Atlantians that were good escaped in many cases and saved their lives by going inside. The lamorians who were warned about it would go to the moon and aslo inside our own earth and created whole cultures and civilizations which they still exist. They have contacted usually those who usually look like them. From time to time they would send embassaries up to communicate to the people that they feel would be able to genetically operate on a higher frequency and can take the strength. Many people are properties and they have already been stamped. That's what we call our birthmarks. Sometimes you see interesting stampings on the body. And you will find that the same satmpings will be on an Asiatic, will be on an African, will be on a Caucasian. And yet there are different races, genetics, and have different dialects. Its because their skin was already stamped and certain souls were put into them. One of the thing s that's happening now is as our sun changes frequency, our inner sun is also changing frequency. It is changing to a point where people who cannot raise vibrations will no longer be able to stay on the surface and they must go home. They must go to those who first propagated them. And they must then be altered or they have to be taken off the planet or they will have to come out of the bodies. This is why death is much different than what we have been told and many people will experience death because those souls cannot go into the new age. One of the blessings and choices given is that people who have been called will be given a gift to the gods. It means again that you are an old soul and you have that privelage. That gift to the gods is again melanin. If you can hon-

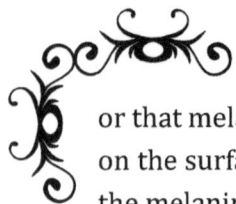

or that melanin, you not only can go into the inner world, but you can go on the surface wherever you want as long as you don't alter or destruct the melanin or the cites which we call cells or the glands and the organs that can take that melanin in. Because automatically we will raise frequency and will match whatever frequency is coming from the inner sun as well as the outer sun. Gravity of course is a prduct of the inner sun pushing against what is called the vortex field of the outer sun and once you can understand taht and build plates that can hold these energy antigravity machines will fill the air as they are. The reason why there is more energy in the earth than you can ever get from the sun or from petroleum, is because the energy is being pushed out constantly to the breathholes of our earth the north pole nad the south pole. The South Pole and constanly screaming around in the energy fields. One of the things I want to say here now and make it very clear what you are not taught is vortex and vortexia. And without that kind of phenomena which you can take or leave. But at least ill explain it to you. You cannot explain gravity, you cannot explain the storms that are coming, or most other things that are happening on our planet. And that concept is simply this that what we call gravity and storms and so on like this is a principle by which most planets and systems are built. It is called a vortex field or vortexia. Vortexia means that if our planet is here, instead of being in orbit.

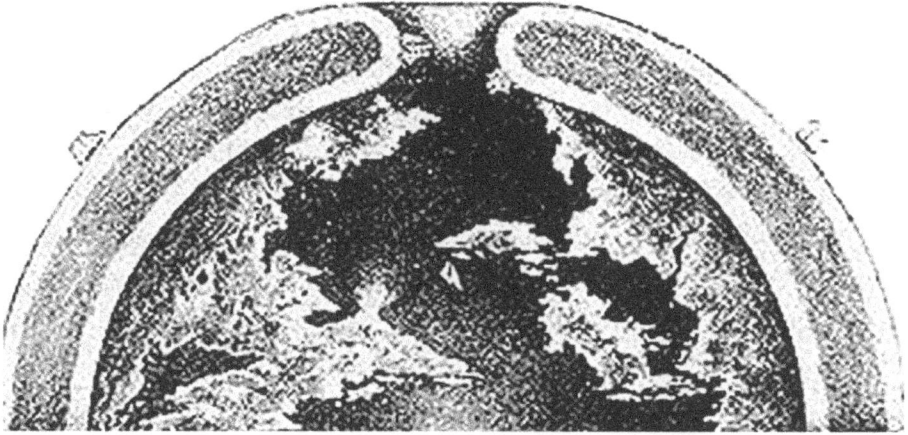

The World Within
Part 1-2

ehind our sun as we are taught and stuff and constantly spiraling all like this with the sun rising and having an axis tilt. We are actually in what is called a vortex which is like a double pyramid. But it is not the same like an equilateral triangle pyramid, it is more curved like a flame and our planet is within it. This vortex field either spins from left to right or right to left depending on the vortex and the planet. All planets have their own vortex. Our sun has a major vortex, which encompasses the vortex of all planets. Let's just say that these planets are all in orbit. Let's say that this is a huge sun here. And of course this is all just exaggeration. And that the sun vortex more or less is like this. So that all planets are in a field or a vortex with their own little vortex no matter where they are in position and orbit around our sun. These vortex fields stabilize the inner sun of planets with the outer area of adaption. The area again by which they are influenced. And this sun has a huge vortex which now when they cross has been called lay lines or magnetic field grids. These things create what is called gravity. It is very easy once you learn how to produce your own little vortex around something to then be pushed away by one sun from a planet, caught up in the gravitational pull of another one pulled to it. The whole idea of it is not how to travel, put the point is how again to get in the frequency because each planet has a different frequency. Our planet is changing frequency at its poles so therefore you are going to see a lot of aurora borealis, your going to hear more and more sightings of things of things coming out of the earth. Because one of the things that they do is that if there is intelligent life is not to contact the surface people who they realize simply what can I say creations. They contact the real intelligent life in Zimbaba, Argatha, or the inner earth. That's why they are usually seen at certain latitudes and they are always making their way to either a cave entrance if its big enough under the ocean where they can hide or go down. And there are crab called yamanas that are used by the people inside the earth and sometimes called ventlas used by people that are on the orbiting satellite which we call our moon. All planets that have moons have automatically intelligent life, because they

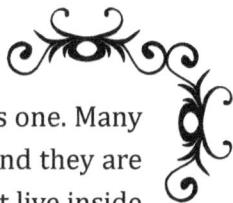

were put up to stabilize that kind of life. And Ill end with this one. Many of the people that made contact from here are from Mars. And they are from Mars because there is a large continent of Martians that live inside our earth and have always had intercourse with you might as well say people here. Once they reached certain vibrations they were taken way to what is called Massa of Mars. The reasons why now they have found a pyramid in Mars because it was shown to them finally the same people that are here are on Mars also. When they found black people on Mars they wanted to stop the whole show. When they found that black woman was the progenitor of original life as well as Mars they couldn't handle it. And this is why you now see maratian probes and why they don't want to take a close up view of the Martian sphinx, because it is a sphinx of a black woman. And it looks that way just as the sphinx out in Giza was too. They are having to fight a battle about who will control the first thee levels of the underworld which has been cleared out as way to hide if these fields of energy become too intense and they do start dropping out chemical bombs and weapons. Nothing chcemical can stay the same once it crosses the poles because they have one of the best air cleaners around. So even if the energy is there to go near the poles you can survive simply because its clean there. But the vibrations of the planet will change there first which means that to go there now is to commit suicide because the vibrations would kill you. You will have a heart attack or your blood would congeal and so on like this. So we are at a point now of mutating once again. And this is far as I want to take this one tonight. I think that I have covered enough territory to create a lot of concentration and questions. I will only say this, there is no truth till you decide what truth is. And this is no more than the fairy tales that you have been told in school for a long time about our planet earth. I thank you very much and give me some applause if you will. It takes the great libraries which told about this phenomena, which were told on parchment and books again cuz they had printed words and even had discs that could be played through an electromagnetic field that were set up again when people got smart enough to be able to use them. And they found these

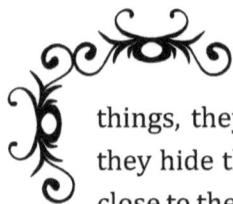

things, they found other ways to get some of the information off and they hide the information. The stanzas from the book of diezen still tell close to the truth. It is one of the people believed in by popula, the people down in Greece and South America. Because they told about the dracons, they told about the prodigies of the dracons, they told about the serpent people and the inside and how they came to their own. And of course you have many of these stories and legends about veranchoocha, ah about all of these gods that look funny and different. Everybody is not fom the same creator. That's one of the biggest lies ever told. Every sole may come from a central creator but the gods differ. And some peoples gods you would not want to be opened. Some people's gods you might want to worship but it would be strictly through fear. And that's why again we have such an amalgamation and so so many things that people find that are different. The gift of the gods in the underworld lets say a person by the name of Seth was melanin. And melanin was given to a body, whichever type of body it was that the soul chose to inhabit would be able to change vibrations and to change frequency. Vibrations and frequency, those are the things to remember now. And that each cell contained itself without bursting and rupturing and change that frequency and that the person soul stay in which we call life.

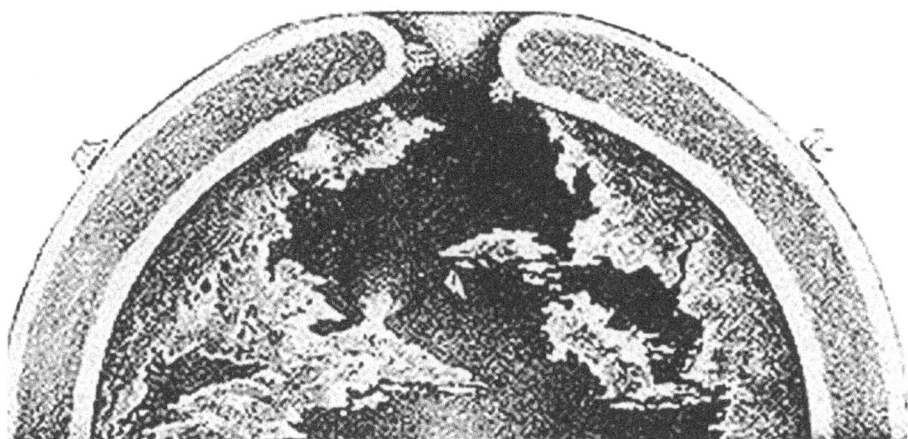

The World Within
Part 2-1

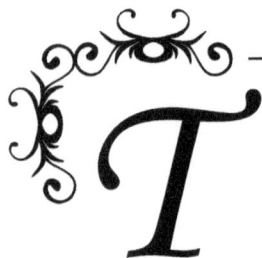

*T*he Meta center wishes to thank you for purchasing this tape directly from the metacenter. The proceeds help keep our doors open and bring the latest in mind body and metaphysical research directly to you. The title of the lecture you are about to hear is called part 2 inside the earth, life forms, technologies, and cities. It was given on Saturday March14th, 1998. In this tape you will names and locations of caves, cities, the central hollow earth life forms, some of their technologies, cave world central city, the ancient montaug alaphabet, and many many more. Interesting and fascinating facts. Hear for yourself. Again Dr. Blair is the director of the metacenter. The metacenter's mailing address is 1448 E. 52nd St, Chicago, IL 60615. Our phone number is area code 773- 643 – 5053. If you are interested in additional audio or video tapes, health products, magnets, diodes, or a personal consultation, please contact the metacenter. Again our phone number is area code 773- 643-5053. Dr. Blair is also available for lectures too. The lecture today is called the world within part 2, life forms, technology, and cities. There is a lot of research involved in this whole series called the world within or the truth about the inner world. Some of the research is done from the smoky god by emerson, the hollow earth by Dr. George Bernard, the savor mysteries by Richard savor, the holy tabernacle scrolls by melachi York, the earth chronicles by zacharia sitchen, subterranean worlds inside the earth by timothy green Beckley, your becoming a galacatic human by Virginia assen and Sheldon nickels, the prisons of lyre, expiration of human galactic heritage by lisa royal and keith priest, and some of the ones that's very hard to get the flying saucer mysteries and shaver mysteries where they ceased to stop publishing back in 1976 with the photos of the essa whole at the pole and many other things that are coming from. There has been over 35 years worth of research to bring this information to you and this is why it is in depth and in many parts. And even with that we probably wont cover all of the subjects because were going to attempt to talk about not only about how earth got populated and came about being, but all the planets in this solar system and all the things that are happening inside of our

planet. The question that has been raised for many a time has been questions that usually go unanswered about what is happening on our planet, why are certain things generally going on. Some of the strange earth questions are the following: Why is it that the north wind of the artic gets warmer as one sails further north or beyond seventy degrees latitude? Another question, why are there warm northerly winds and and an open sea for hundreds of miles north 82 degrees latitude and there are no icebergs there , were going north. After one reaches 82degrees latitude, why is it that the compass of the needle is always balking, agitated, it wont stay fixed on a one unit direction. Again why are there fresh water icebergs and drinkable water within those icebergs in saltwater oceans in all of the areas of our planet where saltwater exist and icebergs exist among? The icebergs are fresh water the oceans are saltwater. How does it get that way? Why is it that anyone can find tropical seeds, plants, and trees floating in the freshwater in icebergs when they melt. And they even have found mammoths, all kind of things that are supposed to be non existant and creatures with green foliage in their mouth still fresh frozen inside of icebergs in salt terrain. Why is it that millions of tropical birds and animals, migrate north even from Bafan Bay, Saskatchewan, Canada, Greenland during the cold season when it is supposed to get colder. Why is it that they found red, pink, yellow, blue, green and assorted color snows in the Artic oceans and the Antartic oceans and on the Antartic shelf. In other words where are these kind of red, green, pink, and blue color assorted snows coming from when you way north or you go way south? Why is there more pollen and flowers on the northerly winds coming from our poles than on tropical winds and other winds coming from the equator. Why is there no proof that any explorer ever reached the north or South Pole? And if you notice now they are bringing back a new thing about perry and bird in a series and they are even now showing now for black history month Matthew Henson. They will even introduce Matthew Henson if it ever makes you believe they discovered the poles. Why are there no polar flights by any of the world's air craft or the world's government and when they put up two satellites the essa 1

sattelite back in 1970 and the essa 3 and 7. There are actually three of them, not two. They didn't go over the poles because when they went over the poles, they were shot down or they crashed. I say shot down because they mysteriously crashed. Now the airline piolots will tell you that they go, have polar flights. They do not. They have circumpolar flights. They go near the poles, they go near 82 degrees latitude and they curve around and go around that pole and go over it. They don't have polar flights. Why is it that down pilots during the worlds wars or if something just happened to happen to their planes while fighting for survival in supposedly the artic ocean and the antartic ocean actually had to battle sand storms so they went further north. Sand storms not snow storms. What really is the cause of the aurora borealis? We have been told that the aurora borealis again is the magnetic flux of energy from the sun with all of the winds and ionic winds that are at the North Pole. Doesn't hold forth, when other things are said. And why is it that the satellites confirm that the earth is flattened near the poles, not like a round ball. But that the earth seems now to be a doughnut than it actually is a circle or a spheroid. All of those questions can be very easily answered, if you believe in what the eskimos say. The Eskimos which are a very interesting people, the look part Chinese, they look part Negroid, they look part asiatic, and they are very short like pygmies if you would and their hair and skin differs. They all say one thing when they asked where do they come from. They say they came form the north. They say well how can you come from the north? You've lived on the ice, on the floats, and on the icebergs. They say no. Their ancestors came from the north and the further north you get, the more climatized it gets, the more easy and balanced the seasons are. This is what they claim. If we also take into consideration as we talked about last week or our last session that the earth may not be rounded at the poles, that the north and south poles may have never been discovered becasuse there is a belief by some that the north and south poles do not exist. As I showed you on that topographical globe before, it simply means you go so far north and you actually start inside the earth because it's a statement that the earth is hol-

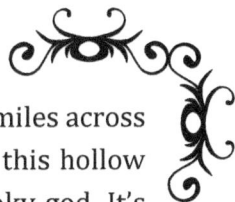

low. That the earth has an area inside roughly around 1700 miles across and its usually about 850 miles through the shell to get to this hollow interior. And inside there is another sun. Its called the smoky god. It's kind of a reddish orange there. By which things that are inside can receive light and heat and that theres green vegetation in the hollow. But the point that they always seem to always overlook or they don't like to talk about that inbetween that, its just like an onion when your peeling it. Inbetween that are caverns and layers, seven of them. The seventh one is a hollow and there a six cavern layers by which whole cities can be swallowed up in. In which we are going to see today life forms actually exist within some of them very intelligent, much more intelligent than we on the surface. The statement I know make is seeming to be that all planets that have intelligent life under this sun and this solar system the intelligent life does not live on the surface because it is very hard to stay alive and intelligent on the surface of our planets and the solar system, especially with our earth. There are all kind of things that are talked about. The most salient creature is that inside of our earth there are life forms many of which are intelligent again. When we look around our planet there are many areas that have reaked with legend, ah disappearing people, strange things seen, and all kind of camaflauge. When you look at teawhenacow down in South America we find not only the gate of the sun where huge monoliths have been built. And people don't understand who could have moved those great weights. But their also told that people there are very physcic if you will. The whole are is down in South America by which people are said to have seen all kind of strange objects that fly in the sky. You even have an area down in South America by which they have a sign on the side of the road saying this is the UFO landing zone. This highway leads to UFO and all these kinds of things as they make joke about it. But if you also remember there are many things and many of the cultures that talk about strange undertakings and strange areas and where gods or high developed people come from. Amongst the Greek there is the story of Olympus,, Mt. Olympus by which ah they said the gods and the Greeks came from. Again there is mount maru agmongst

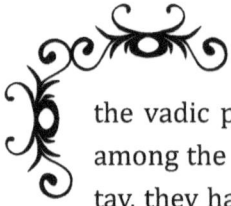

the vadic people. There is called the city of the seven petals of Ishnu among the Buddhists and Brahmen, the egyptains had of course amen-tay, they had the city of the seven kings of eden for the Hebrews if you would, they had aslo the Latin and the Jewish people called the city of eden called the garden of eden if you would the Tibetan and Mohabatan people had shamballah or sham city and allah the city of the king or god, the Persians have alberti or aryama, once they crossover the Hebrew the land of cannon, the Mexican tullah or tollan, the aztecss mayopan, they might say the olmecs, they don't even talk. And most of the time when you hear stories about Mayans they are really talking about Olmecs. The Spanish had el dorado, the aborigines supposedly in Australia and parts of the continent called kem which we now call Africa had minowa, the Celtics had duwat and denada, the chinyans or the Chinese had the land of civen, there is the isle of Baybalon for the British and the Englanders if you would, the Germans had wahalla and they also had the volcarries where the evil portions of those who live in wahalla, and of course the English had what we now call utopia. In the bottom of the Grand Canyon, where ghostwolf now goes, where the United States government wanted to flood recently, because they said they wanted to set up a natural ter-rain, they wanted to restore the Colorado River as it flows through there so tourists could get a better view. You can imagine how about that one. They now find that parts of the Grand Canyon, the water line is now dropping down and these caves down at the bottom of the Grand Canyon now are being exposed. They are being exposed and strange things, lights are coming from them, and sounds are coming from them and peo-ple are saying thay they are seeing strange creatures there. And Lookout Mountain, there has always been stories that deep inside that mountain, that braches into seven paths and nobody knows where they go. Mom-moth cave right down here as you go from Kentucky into Tennesse is also a tourist ground. The legends are that frank james and billie james and so on and so forth during the civil war when the west was won, they used to be able to go inside there and be able to hide their loot and that you could walk from lookout mountain in tennesee all the way to Indiana.

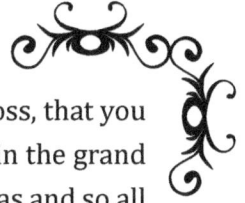

That some say in the Ohio valley all of these tunnels criss cross, that you could go underneath them. Their entrance way supposedly in the grand teetons at Mount Shasta, Lake Victoria in Africa, the Himalayas and so all tunnel entrances leading into what is called cave world. The Cave world is something that you hear all legends about. The talk now and we will be getting more into that next week is that when you start getting into some of these cave worlds, you run into sasquash, yete, abominables that have an awful stench, usually coming anywhere from twelve to fifteen feet tall seem like their Chewbacca like in star wars a good description of what some of these creatures look like. As we will find out they were put there purposely. They are very highly intelligent with heavy karma put there to guard the entrance ways to the underworld. And as people began to now approach the underworld.

As whole platoons of soldiers are now fighting their way into the un-derworld even as we speak world war three has already started. Its not the war that you think. It's the war of weather and the war of regaining the earth. That's what you are living through at this time. All of these creatures are set there to dissuade and persuade people not to take that path. In the rotondo reyez and in the monegroso there are tunnel en-trances that are still open and that's why the monegroso was kept as a verdant jungle to stop any encroachments, now that they are beginning to tear and cut down trees in the montegroso. And just to say that once they do that some of the very air that we are breathing that is still good will be dissipated because of the jungle that was there that acted as ch-lyrophyl, always does cleanse up the air. There cutting that down now, not just for tourist attraction, for other reasons but for other reasons that are happening there too. Inside the caves are many structures of cities and edifices or at least that's what the rumor has, that's what the legenda have always been. But, we'll start off first of all because most people seem very interested in what kind of life form may live inside the earth. Were going to list a few of them again. Going down about 85 miles deep, within the United States, especially again also near the island of

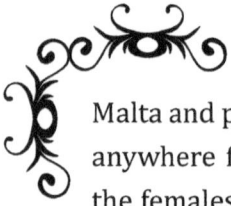

Malta and places are people that are called brilya. Vrilya are large people anywhere from eight feet to tweleve feet tall. Some of them especially the females, have wings. The wings look leathery if you would and they are spindly.

These particular people are said to use vril as their constant force for energy. They would take vril like we are now taking noni or eating this fruit. The only trouble was now that they have extra glands that we don't have and they are capable of flight. They are capable of flight because the wings unfortuantley are not real wings. They are wings that can be attached, because they have large back muscles and underarm deltoids muscles and so. And they develop this over years because they were people who learned to fly emulating the animals of the earth and the birds of the earth. In this area here they have a forest that is called vril which is capable of doing many things not only is it capable of building like steroids would, huge muscular, helping their brains to be utilized better. It also can be used as a weapon. It is a forest that can become liquid and actually can melt rock or when it gets on it can be like an acid and began to destroy it depends again on what they use. Vril is the same thing that's in the book called The Cunning Race by Edward Bulluwar Leton, one of which Caiser Willhiem and Aldolf Hittler studied vehemently. It talked about even a society in Germany and Austria that was called the luminous lodge or the vril society, which believed that many of them incarnated into the german race. I better say that they actually bred and abducted many of the German people and austrain people and mated with them to make them part of this society. And it is one of the secret societies that both Germany and the Illuminati and the Triallateral Commission believe in.

The Stance Union with the three prong trident and is called the Vril society. Down there also as you now go anywhere down to thirty miles down into the earth if you would they have what you call deroes, deroes acronym deroes have many different titles. One deragutaory, degenerate, disrobitized, dis or d- i – s simply means something that disintegrates,

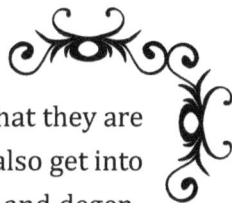

it means something on a downward slope. They have also what they are called energy units from the abondero. The abondero as we also get into next week will be a people who are abandoned on the earth and degenerated. They were like as they say gods that came from outer space. Gods simply meaning they were advanced and scientfic people very advanced in science possibly now at least a good fifty, sixty thousand years ahead of us. That shows just how far they had come that abandoned some of their own here when the radiation fields around earth change. We will get into that next week. But just to show you where they started from. And being abandoned and understanding that they could not live on the surface they burrowed deep into the earth with wonderful tunningbor machines in addition to the natural openings from the gasses of earth that were there when the earth was made. They then began to live all around our earth, under the oceans of our earth, under every continent of our earth, and they have a whole society of people, most of them began to go crazy or mad or at least paranoid from the disintegrative energy that came through. We will get more into that. But that they lived there whether it is a fact or not it is believed in by millions of people and they do bad things.

They also have various devices that they use, which we will be getting into to begin to control peoples mind from a distance. Sometimes they also control animal life and so to have them steal people and bring them to them and they even what they call pairs of the underworld by which gangs that understood their being in Sicily and New York city itself and parts of the United States would actually be paid money through a embassary to have people kidnapped and brought to them, especially women if you would. The United States government also got involved with them. And many of the so called greys that you hear did not come from Jada reticular or aldarbarron as we will talk about next week. They came right inside the earth, they had these degenerate greys that had been here longer than we have. Again as a people or a society they are very negative, they have all types of won-

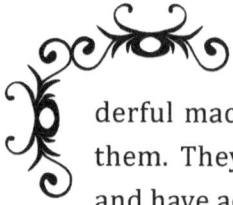

derful machinery that was left over when their parents abandoned them. They are now probably about into the twentieth generation and have adapted to the underworld of earth. Many of the things that have been called trolls, that have been called leprauchauns, and we are about to get into that on St. Paddy's day. And Ill give you that story there too tonight. These things are nothing more than these degenerate robotized individuals that are now part of earth, that were never born of earth that were spawned of earth when scientists goofed. Which shows again no matter how you progress its still capable of making error. Amongst there were also things called teroes. Teroes are ones who have fought the radiation, who have not gone as bezerk as these other ones have, they were from the same source but they has to keep some part of humanity, some part of civilization.

They fought with them but found out that they were losing because many of the teroes became deroes as this disintergrative energy went through their blood they still held out. And it means again simply a more positive or the t square tao force that's where one of the symbols of the cross comes from. For a more benevolent type of energy unit for a person, an energy, or a life form to live down there amongst them and does battle with them. Now more or less tries to help people who unfortunately get caught up in some of their masses.

They have machines down there that can travel at the rate of 2400 miles per hour and they can zoom any where around the earth in one day's time. Understand again about when we are talking about the cave world, inner world or underworld we are not just talking about one level like we are on the surface of ours. We are talking about six different levels. Each one capable of supporting life, each one with major cities like the onion as you go deeper and deeper. Another type of creature that is seen down there is this thing called hyperbeings. And that'sn acronym used by some and others call them hyperborans. Either way you are talking about the same place. The legends have that at the antartic area there was a continenet where people called hyperborans.

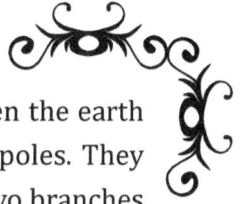

These hyperborans again went inside the earth also when the earth began to be so disentigrate that radiation collected at the poles. They were forced inside the earth also. Many of them represent two branches the numos, that's n – u- m- o-s or the reptilian. Some say the numos are reptilian. I say that they also may be snake creatures. Their called the word numos which means law givers. There was a numos that contacted again the dogans in South Africa in Mau, they are dealing some serious speed. They came to the dogans again out of water and because they had an amphibious background they could not stay on the land during the daytime in the sunlight.Thy do not like sunlight. They have now by the way adapted. Don't go by those old legends anymore. They have adapted now to just about everything. But at the beginning they were the ones who saw people the dicillaries, the twoaregs, the dogans in Africa, they are the ones that were approached by this creature that they said was a helpful creature from them. It came from Siruis. So believe me agin, not only do you find Orion nasty, but there are some parts of sirius. Let me state another thing, siruis is not a binary star as we have been taught. There are actually three stars in siruis. Sirius A, Siruis b, and Siruis C.

They still haven't discovered the third one and that third one is a counteracting agent between siruis A and Siruis b. They have not only lived beneath the continent of Africa, but they have now spread to any-where where they have underground rivers and waters or where they can reach the surface. The story of the creature from the black lagoon is a real one. The only thing was at the first time when they were first degenerative they were not so tall, some of them have grown taller now, but some of them were more or less four or five feet tall. Some of them were pink, some of them were green, some of them were grayish black. They were simply a cross between a reptile if you would or an amphib-ious reptile and a humanoid if you would. There is another one called olnomo. Olnomo difference from the new nomos again. It means of the pond, they are strictly water creatures. They do not go onto the land, if they go onto land its for a short short time.

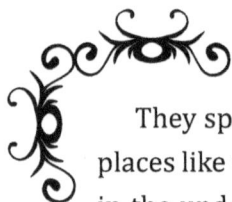

They spend most of their time in either pond water or in lagoons or places like this. In short there are sixteen types of reptilians that can live in the underworld. I like to call it the innerworld of the caveworld, including a reptilian that looks like a gargoyle. They are the ones that don't have attached wings like the real people. They will grow wings if you would. The stories of vampires come from the stories of the gargoyles or these underneath there. Many of them call them v for Vulcan vampires. The word vampires stands just like the movie is showed for v. That's why that movie is shown about every six years for the last forty five years. It will be on again in the fall. This time was a whole different twist to the plot. Plus they had coupled with the series again based on v. V is for Vulcan where they came from a moon on Vulcan and also a is for the Vulcan empire. Again even star wars was based on the trilogy that talked about the Vulcan Empire. Now we are seeing that the gargoyles, one of their offshoots live there. They also are found in the Ohio Valley. Beneath the Ohio Valley roughly about five miles down there is a peat moss that has never been put out.

It keeps everything down there very warm. If ever there was an implosion in the Ohio Valley, which means Ohio Pennsylvania, parts of New Jersey, places like that, that whole area would just explode because there is a hot layer roughly around three miles down from peat moss close to three miles dedep and going on for at least two thousand miles in a mandering circle that is always warm. They actually have these creatures that live down there. There is an old book they call the silver bridge and the silver bridge will tell you all of the people that were kidnapped just like they are doing now. All of the strange sightings of these winged creatures and they even collapsed a silver bridge there in Pennsylvania roughly around 1967. When a formation flew over and two of them had been captured and killed and the whole bridge began to tremble because they let out some kind of sound like sonar sound. The bridge collapsed. It killed close to a thousand people. It was hushed up, because not only did the cars fall during rush hour, but they fell into the water crushing ships

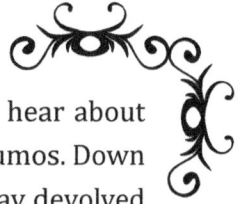

and so on like that. It is called the silver bridge. If you will hear about that one again. But they are again part of what you call the numos. Down there also are trolls. They have devolved or degenerated, I say devolved from what I call trabludites or Trojanian, the Trojan horse now with a j now with a g, Trojans.

They live also underneath the sea and in even deeper layers of the cave world, because again they can stay in the water and they now can of course, they have all mutated. But what they wanted to do since it was more of a fish type creature and pretty soon next week we will tell you why so many things are here on this planet. There is a definite reason and well deserving so. They actually mixed with what they call humans and they mated with humans. And they kept their spawn down there until which time they could also train them to be what they call traubladites and native people which we now call earth. When you start saying people of earth you must understand, everything here is not the same and everything here is not subject to the same diseases, and everything here does not need the same nourishment because they have different mothers and fathers even though we are all lumped together and we call ourselves human beings or earth people if you would. There are amazing technologies that exist in this cave world. There is something that is called plasmic energies.

The best thing that I can say abpout plasmic energy is that they are liquid like coming from highly condensed energy.Liquid like coming from highly condensed energy. Some of the fireflys that we see and sometimes the luminous light that you see when they put these two chemicals together there is a little globe that comes in there. Well you take that globe and you amplify it with nuclear reactors if you would. And you can begin to get a light that almost becomes a liquid. It can actually be capable of movement like plasma. It can be fired, it can be drained, and it can be used almost in a way you get thick liquid again. They also have what they call photothermic machines and photothermic chemicals if you would. Photothermic is the idea that I can best explain, cuz these are all differ-

ent kind of technologies now. Beside their providing a source of light and heat from the abrogation of light frequencies. They are able to bend light, they are able to cut down the frequencies or step up the frequencies of light so that it can began to produce friction for heat and luminescence from the actual agents that they are actually smearing on. This means that the caves down there can be lit up.

Theres a glow that can come. Where there is darkness now you have light, of you would. They have this on most of the underground caverns and tunnels. It is simply called photothermic chemicals or photothermic plasma. They also have something that is called photovoltaic energy. Photovoltaic, this is an idea of providing a source of electric current from light or similar radiations like light. It is really something that is called the frequencizing of light and radiation into electrical energy. We get ours from turbines, the power that is released by swiftly turning an object and then you get a power. This is made by emploding or fusing together light and radiation.

Light and energy sources and then being able to focus it out. You don't have to have carrier lines for this. You beam it out or it can be sent through the actual earth itself because in most of the earth there is what they call presoic electricity, little glass molecules, little crystal molecules all in the earth itself, which are excellent conductors. And by the way they bored these tunnels. They actually fused this energy creating what they would call natural pockets of quarts and natural pockets of crystals which then can be used for illumination. This is why they got an inner luminescence. Now we haven't even talked about the inner sun but we are talking about these caves are now warm and they can have light using these whole different new concepts again. They have things there that are called if you would exd rays. That's exd rays, they have what they call stem rays, and they have what they call bin rays. This is again based on this ability of genegrating energy through liquid light and fusing again atoms until they give off light. And having some kind of sound or beam to push that energy through.

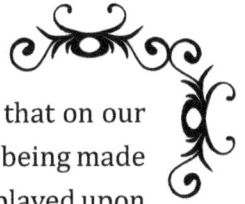

This is the best I can say it because we have nothing like that on our surface or at least we didn't. I don't know now with the deals being made what may be secret weapons again. A stem ray is a ray when played upon the human body works on a chakra center, which then they will work on all the glands of the body. It stimulates the person into ecstasy or into corruption whichever. It's a constant ray which they call a stem ray, which can speed up healing twenty five times faster than anything we have that can heal by simply passing this ray over. Wombs can begin to heal automatically, bones grow overnight. The stem ray is what they call a bin stem ray. Bin meaning good ray.

They aslo have what they call exd rays, which ar every harmful. They can chop you up, they can melt you. They can do anything else any of these rays do. It's almost the same the brill society use, only on a much higher level. They got there as we will find out, it was a gift or a curse from the gods at one time or another. Again when I say gods im not talking about any religious gods. Im talking about adavanced scientific thinking people who to us wouold be godlike because of the science that they have. The science either that we have forgotton or have never had. These rays can be used as what they call shorter rays where they can short circuit your energy fields and every molecule in your body begans to disentigrate. This is where you hear the story of spontaneous combustion, where people just burn up and their clothes are untouched. That's the bin rays. These kinds of rays can penetrate and they won't even touch metal or wood, they touch flesh and blood. And your clothing won't be singed but your burned from the inside out. Somebody puts a shorter wave, short circuits your electromagnetic unit cause they call this units of consciousness. It short circuits our consciousness and our physical being. This is a whole different kind of weaponry.

This is where people with spontaneous combustion its nothing spontaneous. Somebody puts a bin ray on them or else gave them what they call liquid plasma in their food and they began to melt from the inside out. This is also a place where they use levylift beamers. Leavy lift beam-

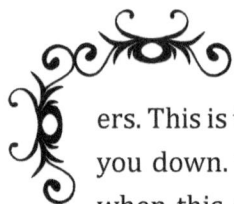

ers. This is the thing like in star wars they beam you aboard or they beam you down. They have a tractor leveylift which can then levitate you up when this ray goes down. It grabs hold to all of the electrical conduit within the body. The little energy fields around all cells. As you know all of our cells have two electrons spinning. It grabs hold to one of them shorts again, raises the vibration, and person lifts stuff each body. The terrible thing about that if you have a lot of flesh or you have a lot of energy that can't be easily transformed, it can also disintegrate you in the process of lifting you up.

That's why everbody can't be lifted up by what we call these levylift beamers. As they put it on you otherwise it's just like a shorter ray or somebody put a raybeam on you and you died or melted again from the inside out. They have what they call tellavs. Its close to what we have now called television, only amplified 50,000 times. These tellav can send out selenoid projections much like what we call holograms and they can put within that a soul or energy field where that thing will not only then be put there but it can move through walls or anything else. Its on a tellav beam but they can actually use this tellav beam to have this person, creature, or thing act or actually do harm or do good. It is nothing but a seleniod projection from a tellav beam but when a person sees it they think that the thing that they are seeing is real and it can touch them, it can even electrocute them, it can heal them, it can hurt them. And you can begin to imagine some of the things you have heard about if they have such a beam, weapon, or what they call a tellav beam.

Were approaching it now with holograms. But our holograms right now can't actually touch you. They can perform for you and you think that they are there. A tellav machine can send a hologram that can destroy you, help you. It can beam any relatives that you have because they also heve on the tellov beam memeory readers, which means that they can use your thoughts and they can synchronize your thoughts. Make you think you see whatever it is you think you see. Think about that. They make you think you see whatever you think they see. Now that's

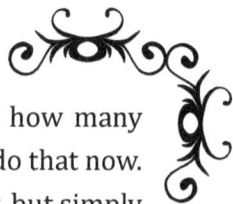

what you call where holograms will go maybe in the next how many thousand years. But there are a force on our planet that can do that now. Many of the mibs are not real mibs unlike the movie you saw, but simply tellav machine replicants when a person sees a UFO or gets too close to a government installation or too close to some of the things that they send out. You think you see it and it can hurt you and it can help you.

In many cases its helped people. But it's called a tellav machine with levylift beamers and so on again like that. There are many other technologies some of which I don't even know about. But you can imagine if they can do these kinds of things with these machines, how valuable they are. As we will find out too, those machines still await some people's usage because they have been protected for usage by people on the planet earth when they reach a certain vibration.

Another gift from the gods we will be talking about that next week. So its not all bad. Its not that you can't be taught to use it too its just that nobody ever trained you. Like how many people have actually gone to a gun range and practiced every month or every week and so on that. What you don't use, you cannot use. What you don't use, you will loose. Such has been thecase of what has been the legacy that was left for earth itself. There is a language that is generally used amongst people now and we have been told that the tower of babel, the languages of earth were confused, so that man would not be able to come as god or as those multitudes of things that were called gods or as the creator.

We have been told that the tower of babel, this is biblical of course that everything that we did then was confused so that the tongues of man and the tongues of mankind would not be that could understood. They would not seek to be as the Gods that were above them. This is interesting because there is a language spoken down by many of these creatures called the mantong language. M- a – n – t – o- n – g. And it constitutes what is called the mantong alphabet. Mantong alphabet, mantong language. That was first brought out in what was called the shaver mysteries or the hidden worlds put out by zift publications ceased to publish again

after 1967 when Ray Palmer in Wisconsin died. But stated within there again, there is a whole alphabet by which many of the letters in our own English alphabet and in the romance languages portugese Spanish Latin again were utilized again.

Each one of those letters stood for a symbol if you would and the mantong alphabet if you would was also said to be used by those that once you begin to augment yourself and grow in consciousness that you would be able to then think these symbols through and that this was a way of telepathy. They used symbos for words or signs as we now hear one picture is worth a thousand words was a way of beginning to speak that would help those who had a higher frequency form pictures in their minds, which could be thought read, especially using tellav machines and memory recorders. There is also, there is so much that I want to share with you here that um.

There are many refernces to the underworld, and I only use this because many people are very bible oriented and because of this they say well if these things exist why does the bible speak of it and the book of revelations, the book of joeb, the book of enoch and so have said many things but why aren't they there. I want to quote you some scriptures from some from these passage ways or passages that might make you think that this was referred to again. Before the flood in Noah's days the earth was said to consist of sixth seventh land and only one seventh water from the book of essrah sixth chapter fourty second verse. The canopy of frozen water existed above the atmosphere and the entire world enjoyed an even cool temperature. Genesis 1st Chapter seventh verse, tropical planets, trees, and animals, and birds were just as plentiful at the north and south poles of the equator.

The word Eden means a delightful region or abode that is paradise as you want to succumb to know. The Garden of Eden was in the eastern part of Eden genesis second chapter eighth verse. Now when Adam and Eve supposedly disobeyed the lord, they were driven out of the Garden of Eden and the lord placed chermons and a flaming sword to keep them out, gene-

sis third chapter, twenty fourth verse.Nothing was said about keeping holy angels or evil angels out of Eden inside the earth. In fact it is said that Satan and his angels were cast out of heaven into not onto but into the earth. And before Adam was created seven references to the bottomless pits more or less include that Satan's angels are still in the abyss inside the earth.

That's revelations ninth verse second chapter eleventh verse seventh chapter, seventeeth verse, sixth and twentieth chapter first verse, third chapter. The earth we are told is constantly turning, therefore there is spot in the earth that can be called bottom. Therefore the great deep space or bottomless pit abanon would have to be seven thousand miles across. And because it has no bottom, of course your talking about now inside the hollow, what has been called the sides of the beast or the sides inside the tuma. There are several bible verses that I think again might prove that fallen angels are down under the earth.No man in heaven and earth, neither under the earth was able to open the book, neither to look up thereon, revelations fifth chapter third verse.

Every creature in heaven, on earth, and under the earth were saying grow in power, be onto the land, revelations fifth chapter, thirteenth verse. In Jesus name every knee will bow with angels in heaven, men on earth, and angels under the earth, second chapeter tenth verse. God spared not the angels that sinned but cast them down under in tarterless to be reserved until judgement, Ephesians part 2, and second chapter fourth verse. The evil angels he has reserved in age lasting change under the earth for judgement of the great day. What does ju stand for, sixth chapter? Genesis no that would be g. I have to go back to that one. Judgement, Jeremiah, probably judgement. Judgement sixth chapter. Jesus ascended, but he ascended first into the lower parts of the earth, they say again to preach to evil angels, ephisians, fourth chapter, ninth verse, Matthews, tweth chapter, fourtieth verse. The angels come to mean more or less messenger or agent. There are over three hundred bible verses that speak about angels and they may be of course many thousands of years old and accepting for two differences. The cherabum and a seraphin. All angels are actually people or men or

beings if you would. Some of them are highly evolved celestial beings and we will find that next week. Some of them are not so evolved. But at the same time on this planet they exist. Where do they exist?

The statement is inside the earth. Enoch if you remember salt paradise in the earth. From chapter seventeen to chapter sixty five of the book of enoch, you read about the beauty and the grandieur of the interior of the earth. That's seventeen to sixty five in the book of enoch. They also tell about the awful deep valley that are there, the sides that are there, the tremendous house in mountains, and you saw trees there taller than any tree you have ever seen on earth., and wider rivers which many colorful flowers so on like that. Of course you remember enoch also walked with god and translated and was no more. He met up with a mighty angel that took him off or whatever way you wish to interpret it. There are many things that are said about also the cities that are within the earth. Most of those things became hush hush but the legends of some of which will recognize as I go through them again. One is called rainbow city. Rainbow city is found in the antartic near where we propose this concept and this text today is near going into the inner earth itself going into the sides of the south, not just the sides of the north. Rainbow city therefore is near the South Pole.

It's therefore on the antartic continent past the royal shelf. The entrance there as we get near it supposedly has very high walls of ice. Some of the ice is plastic. It is not real ice, but seems to be if you climb over or are in that particular area. Some of them 10,000 feet high almost forming a valley for what is called rainbow city again. Many of the bright colors that make up these plastics and have iridescence and some plastic that has been infused with color are from bright red and orange to bright green purple and yellow and when the sun light hits them just like when you see sunlight on the snow here, itt's a beautiful thing. Its seems to cascade a rainbow like prismic effect. And people have seen this in flying near the South Pole have wondered what that was.

It's called again rainbow city. At one time was occupied by people in

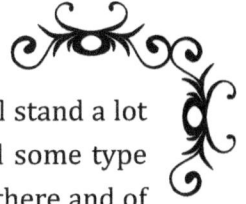

space who did not want to go inside the earth but could still stand a lot of light and they built these cities of endurable plastic and some type of other fusing material which I have no idea. But it stands there and of course it blends right in with the ice and people will look at it as a plastic or ice contained city. It is said to be inhabited now by many beings from earth human beings and also a kind of advanced beings from the inside of earth. And this is where we will finish off inside the earth and the hollow earth. Also, people that talked about the ancient three. Which recently the ancient three hit the news a lot of people supposedly killed themselves by transcending when the commit came over. It is said to be talked about by the ancient two.

There is even an older group of people who wanted to catch the commit. Remember about ah hale bob and people out in California again, heavens gate ok, well supposedly he commited suicide. He was the last one that was able to get away from there. One of the rumors that came about there was that these people died in stages, which meant that some people had to kill other people or watch other people die. This is a very hard thing to do before they die. They just didn't die from poison all at once. They died in stages. This man was going to write a book. He had contracts all where he left. He said he did not want to die. All these things you hear on the art bell show and a large response. He is now dead. He killed himself. So now all of them have killed themselves and joined whoever it was and of course the comet is now gone. I guess he just couldn't take all of his friends being gone. On the radio he seemed to handle it very well. And seemed to like the money he was going to make from it.

Now he is dead. Oh yes I listened to all of that. It's almost like poor mcgregor. Anybody remember who mcgregor was? We won't go there then. Well we will leave that one alone for right now. Its interesting also that once you get past the cavern worlds and the cavern cities and there are many of the cavern cities, beneath New York City where many of the so called deroes and things fashion themselves. When they try to live in these great cities and they push dope and drugs and everything else to

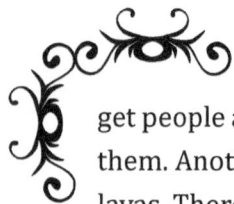

get people and the bodies of people, the spirits of people to be brought to them. Another is called tean city. Tean city or t- e- a-n is near the Himalayas. There is another city that they have there, I cant think of the name of that, dolce. Oh you must stay away from dolce. Dolce not only is where the government of the United States or whatever of government that this is now. I have no idea what the government is any longer. Some of you may know, I don't. But there in New Mexico there is a little town called Dolce. They have huge installations that go from there all the way to the Rocky Mountains underground. And they have at least thirteen known levels, seven that they talk about.

If you remember seventh was called Cora hall. Well in case you don't, let's kind of go into that a little bit. This is an area where the United States Government or the armed forces or whoever again that represents us that supposedly is creatures that look like us that we believe in have gotten a deal going with some of these so called deroes which they now call greys or bphats, by which they are now experimenting with people. They have now done whatever they pretty much want to. They have crossed genetically breed spider people, alligator people, you name it. Ostritch people, frog people, and they have also feed the granular secretions of people, melting them down and fed them to these reptilian greys because they cannot ingest. So they ingest through their pores and through the skin, while working a syrup made up of the glands and things of cattle and people all together boiled down. They not only have that but they have a lot of research facilities there for advanced flying machines and they connect very well with area 51, with areas of the royal teatons by which they are using what they call the aurora project, which is part of area 51. But area 51 now is not this confined area 51.

Some of these planes that they have which are usually triangular shaped and greenwith thhe green phosphorescence can travel 26000 miles an hour. So they can even go to other planets in these same ships if they can get past the magnetic fields. Down there is a place where three kinds of aliens actually live. They are interfaced with people here on

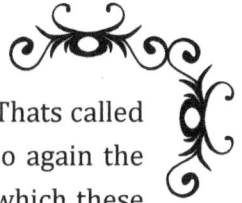

earth and they do a lot of wonderful things as you can see. Thats called Delci. But beneath delci, thirty miles beneath delci, are also again the areas of the ancient ones which were both good and bad, which these people who now came understand that they were there, understand that they were their ancient ascestors and they have a lot of interfacing with. We will be talking about that next week too. That is another city in the earth that you would like to stay away from delci, New Mexico if you would. Looking past now the cavern worlds and now entering into the hollow earth or the concept of the hollow earth, this is where you would find your more benevolent and higher concscious people.

These people have come from as you have heard a place called lamooria, sometimes referred to as lu, sometimes referred to as pan or wagapan, which is wagawackapan is now jaipan or japan. These were people that lived on a continent that we talked about briefly in one of the other classes in a huge area that took up the Pacific Ocean by which now you have just have the top of islands, the hawian islands, Easter islands which nobody can explain. It was a southern portion there where they had a lot of ships there that landed and they did a lot of monument building and so on like that. That's why Easter Island has the monoliths and if you study some of the pictures of Easter islands by the way, instead of looking at the big heads they have, if you look at the mountains themselves they are all sculptured. You see faces in the mountain where they actually or it is resourt area of ancient lu or lemuria.

The people that fled the devastation of lamooria when it broke up and it broke up over a five year period of time. Warnings went out for almost twenty years. And your talking about almost 250, 000 years ago. It was the largest piece of landmass that our planet earth had. Of course you will find next week that there are many other names for earth other than just earth. These people there had a very ancient science and they were pretty much in general a good people overall. They had three different kinds of races. One a kind of a black race, one a brown race, and one a red race. And these were people that came from other planets. We will

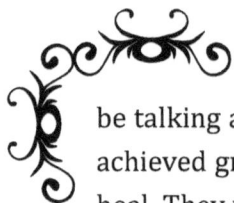

be talking about that and they set up a colony there, unmoved and they achieved great science. They has these bin rays there that were used to heal. They were able through means of telavs to communicate with animals if you would. They were able to use levitating rods to fly with, which the legends of withes came from with broomsticks. They were able to untransmute matter to make it lighter and have it float so that they could move big stones and things around.

They were very psychic with extremely long heads. These are the pygmy type shapes or the giants that were there. And their land went down through a series of catacylsims that were not caused by them. They were caused again by a lot of the gasses that were in the earth and by energy that came from our sun with a reverse polarity. Well talk about that next week. Because of this their land began to break up and its such a huge area that as it was breaking up the final touch was a huge water canopy fell upon it. And that came from the huge destruction that happened in our solar system, where we get the thirteenth planet or triscadecafolia. Something that happened so mighty that it changed the whole course of our planet. This area of lamooria, as the people saw this breaking up, many of them went into kemet, many of them went into the Indian Ocean area. Kemet is now of course Africa. Africa is not the real name of that continent. That's why it has no long history. But when you understand that it was one of the biggest land masses. After lamooria fell they went into there , they went into the area in South American Brazil, they went deep inside the earth beacause they knew of the underground cities and those that would survive had to do this because for a while our earth was almost very radioactive. These lamoorians sometimes called mooains, because another sysnonym or acyronym for lamooria was the mu with the mu called moo. Its been referred to also as I say as pawn. And you hear about the pipes of pawn used to blow chords and sysnchronist vibration to help people's minds to adjust, to kill of germs and bacteria.

Because of the frequency of these horns and the pipes of pan that they could blow. They used harmonics along with light to heal and color

to heal. We just beininning to find how ultraviolet light and infared can now not only hurt as everything here is used for destruction, they can began to help. They used this kind of way and they used it to organize the chakra centers so people heal from within as well as without. There were other things that happened. They had a battle wioth the moon , we will talk about. That's how the pac mark got up there. And agian with all this happening at once, the great land was destroyed and many of them that could not leave the planet actually went inside the earth. So, down there in the central city, by the name of Shamballah, the city of Allah again or actually Shamballa means scented of Allah. The smell of Allah.

This is where many of them lived. They were generally very benevolent. There are now about four different races of people that live down there. Including black people, they are a very tall form of a white person with more of a pinkish or green skin, many of them are actually green and a combination of other creatures that raised higher vibrations including the famous Ashtar and Hatton. Many of you are into that. So, I wont touch that for further than that. But Ashtar and Hatton did not look like what you think. You have heard about rumors, supposedly a reptilian who found the light. But at any rate I must say that there are many creatures there, there is much technology that is there. And they are really what they call the kings of earth.

The king of the world that dwells within it. Many of the Buddhists understand that, many of the shamans understand that, and many of the lamas understand that. One of the reasons seemingly for the Dali lama coming to write pattterson airforce base as did the pope was because they knew that in this year or the next year, people would have to began to learn what was there and what it was going to do to religion and the dali lama said well you already know that. So they asked could he make contact with the king of the world and he is supposed to be the embassary for the king of the world. That's when they had all religions to meet each year, all 129 of them at the Palmer House and the key ones met agin with the whatvever you want to call the United States government.

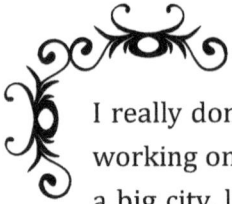

I really don't know how to address them. Ah with whatever forces are working on our planet, this is where they met. In agartha, which is like a big city, lets say that Shamballa is not a city but a continent like the United States. Another key city there is called Argatha. Argatha means through the hole. It's a city reached by going through the hole. You're going through the hole again at the North Pole or at the South Pole. At agartha are also some of the creatures or life forms that come from outer space that go there to keep track of whats happening here. Because they have a huge computer there that keeps track of most of the beings and their whereabouts and all like this.

They also generate new air and help the earth to breathe. Now long ago we would kill ourselves off, it's just a matter of now trying to clean up the ozone. Had that been allowed to penetrate to the inner sun, it would have been an implosion and the earth would have just folded in upon itself. So they have great cleaning machines that are there. In agartha of course also are the what they call ventlas. Ventlas are a form of flying saucer or UFO that comes from inside the earth. It has nothing to do with outer space or other planets. It is a means of vehicle by which they travel through the tunnels. And when they really want to go fast to the moon or nearby areas through these ventlas which land usually in Agartha or in a place called Tellov city. In Tellov City aslo which is beneath Mount Shasta.

Also there are tunnels that lead beneath the great Sphinx and the pyramid. And that's one of things that they don't want you to find. It will have to be open December 12th of this year officially. When the genocins or the people are probably surfaced there and meet some of the Egyptian people because at that time, this government also plans a great confuscious. And so therefore December 12th you might march unless somethings really happen, it will be quite a turning time for this planet. But underneath there they can go to any continent that they want within seconds because they have the trailways or the tunnels that lead there. And this is where they supposedly have giants that still live in the earth. The trees that grow there are very big.

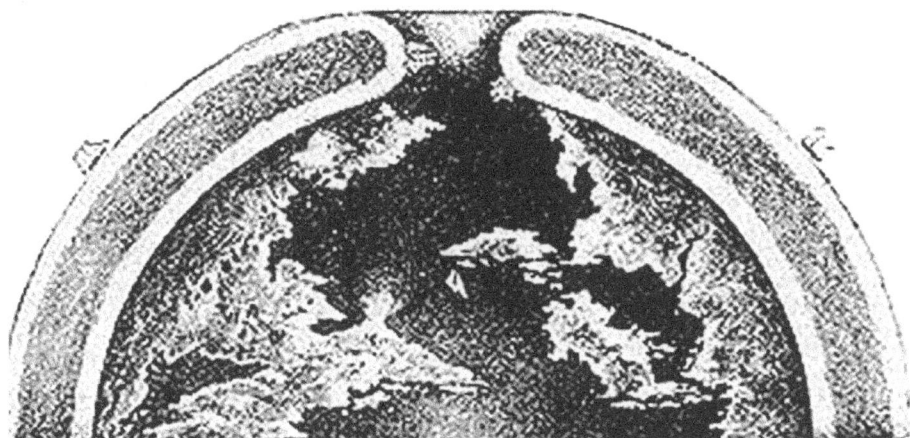

The World Within
Part 2-2

*J*jungles that are there. They have a few of them because they want the life and the oxygen that these things produce. They also have the wooly mamooth that is still there and they have dinosaurs that still exist there. So you don't have to worry about them cloning here at the University of Chicago as they are now doing. At the field museum where they have relic just like in the movie. Thye already have them there and one of the things that has happened is that two of the dinosaurs which they had also replicated were contacted by dinosaurs inside the earth, which are very intelligent and are even now are bipedal. For each thing evolves as it would. And now those dinosaurs or if you would call these platosauruses have attacked United States cruisers and destroyers and the shells bounced right off of them just like in the movies.

They were in the straights of Madagascar and Madagascar Island becasuse in Madagascar Island, there is a mountain that goes into the underworld and they have not only been attacked, of course some of these dinosaurs that were man made and released have now turned back upon their makers. And that's why they are sending out all these sonar things, cause they are afraid that these dinosaurs might come out of the water just like in the movies. That is not supposed to happen but it is a lesson to them who began to go too far with cloning and so as to what can happen. Because those creatures never did leave the earth. They were simply put in quarantine and some taken away and some like t rex by which by the way t rex was a man made monstrosity that they are trying to do again. There was never a beast as t rex. It was a cross between a serpent and a reptile. And actually t rex is what they are trying to clone. Tell me again why if you heard the stories, why would you want to clone and revitalize something that was so desperate and so evil on its flesh highly carnivorous, it would eat itself if necessary just a vicious beast. Why would you want to clone that and bring it back? But them I ask the same question, why would you want to bring back a black plague.

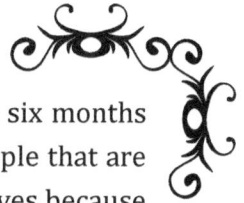

By going to a plague that killed off five million people in six months time and revitalize it. Because there are certain surface people that are being controlled by vinicins that don't want to do it themselves because of karma will let people on the planet do anything that they want to. And they give them certain rewards of pleasure that they love. Very interesting again. So you have down there under control, meaning the beast that we were told were disintegrated or breed out, they are very extinct. They are not extinct. And again one of the secrets that I tell you is that the oceans have serpents that are swimming in pairs that even the giant squids and all are running from. Interesting too let me say that many of the so called fish people and dolphins have a higher vibration than we do. Now I should say a higher vibration than humans that are using them. One of the reasons they are beaching themselves is not only to escape these serpents, but they know that they can reincarnate. And they might now get to reincarnate inside the earth and now go on to bigger and better things.

They don't have the fear of death that we do. So you have a lot going on at this time. Now all of these things are realized as a way out. And I don't expect you to believe all of the things you have heard. I don't even expect you to belive any of the things you have heard. I don't expect anything from you but to listen, which you have done and I thank you. I simply say now use this as a research broach, a material, a reason to not now study and learn and make decisons. Because if any of the things and we have covered so many things tonight quickly to make your head swim. Don't make your head swim. Let your consciousness expand. People that said I just start thinking and I get headaches. That's only the figment of your imagination. We haven't begun to use our brains yet. And if we don't began to use our brains we will not be able to go into the new age because you must think and you must evolve. Your going to have to expand consciousness.

We have so many unused portions and cells in our little cranial areas again, in our little neuron centers and so and so forth till you have to

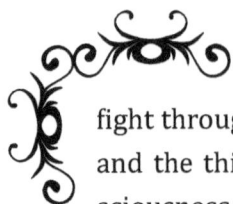

fight through in order to awaken them. And as you take in the solutions and the things that I am telling you about they will expand your consciousness because they will raise the vibrations of the blood , wear out the mucous and the sap that has clogged them up and began to try and fire. So it's no such thing as you can't think. This is nothing compared to supposedly what we can do if we ever activate our pineal gland and as I say as we will be talking about this sun reverses complete polarity as I think it is going to in order toeven stay alive you will have to mutate. Mutation will be in consciousness. Once you mutate in consciousness the body simply assimilates whatever the brain tells it to do. And you know its no problem at all. But if you fight that or if the vibration just cannot go into what is called now the Aquarian age and the higher consciousness, yes you can come down with all kinds of diseases.

So it's much a point of you taking over your own body and helping it to evolve in consciousness to match people who are already inside the earth and again understand this. The folks that we are looking for to help have their own problems. They do have problems, but they will help if it is not too troublesome. They only way they can help you, the ones you want is to raise your vibrations. If you are so low or you stink like a skunk or a dirty dog or like anything else you wouldn't want to help anybody that smelled and neither would they want to help you if you smelled. If your vibrations and consciousness and thoughts are all so unclean then it means that the people that want to help you have to hold their nose and just help you from the goodness of their hearts. Whereas there is certain things now that you can began to do if you are into mediation. Notice again meditation is growing. People are spending time just going within, not just praying toJesus or to Allah.

But spending time also trying to do for self. As you spend time doing that you are thinking thoughts that raise vibration casue these thoughts hae a higher vibration. And the rewards are that your body becomes a higher unit of consciousness or so. Whether there be nortans or what they call blonds, hagman from heckata as we will be talking about, also

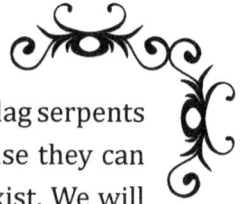

whatever deroes degenerate robotized individuals, gillman, flag serpents and reptiallians or so. All of these creatures are here because they can be here. And if they couldn't be here they would cease to exist. We will find again as we raise our concsciousness and as the vibrational rates of our planet changes into a magnetic field things that can't be here or shouldn't be here wont be here.

It's a matter of thought. But if the main folks , folks who are seated here, folks who live on our planet, the six and a half to seven billion people who are here for a purpose, don't raise their consciousness , then they will have to go elsewhere to do what they have to do. If they can, everything you don't like will soon be separated from you or you will forget and it won't hurt. But if we can't and I say heaven or somebody help us because we will be in for a time. It's been way out. I thank you very much and we are open for questions, statements, and comments.

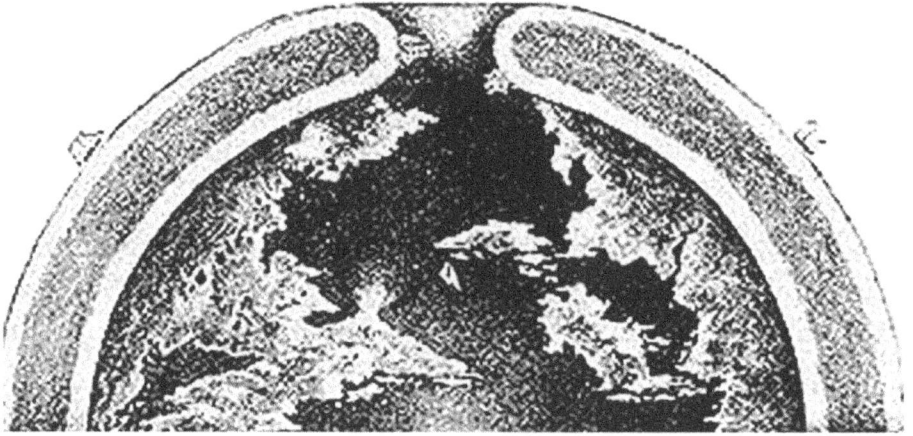

The World Within
Part 3-1

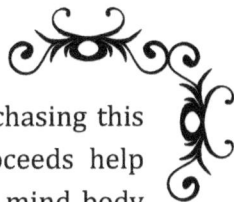

*T*he Meta-Center wishes to thank you for purchasing this tape directly from the metacenter. The proceeds help keep our doors open and bring the latest in mind body and metaphysical research directly to you. The title of the lecture you are about to hear is called the world within series part 3, Ancient History of the Inner Earth. It was given by Dr. Delbert Blair in March 1998. If you are interested in additional audio or video tapes, health products, magnets, diodes, or a personal consulation for your self or your loved ones, please contact us. The lecture entitled the world within part 3; it's called the ancient history of our inner earth.

And the reason why I showed again these things were pulled off of the internet, from the art bell show with Robert ghostwolf was to simply show that there might be a truly cave world that everybody can began to see very quickly by just going to one site. This is one of the reasons why they probably did not publish exactly where this site was. What I am also saying in the years to come and this is starting with this year, youre going to hear more and more talk about the inner earth and the last world and the inner world. The last two sessions that we had and one more after this will be covered in detail so that you get an over view of what is going to be said, what might be happening, and the reasons for it again. These website pictures I think are very beautiful.

Again I would suggest if you want them we can make copies for you or if youhave your own interenet and website and you want to go for it again then you can pull them up yourself. And Ill leave these also up here on the break if you want to take a look at some of the pictures yourself. Yes. Oh the dot com series and all that. I don't right off, I can give it to you again at the break again if youwould like. I want to move on with this one right now though. Oh one other thing that I have here, it shows what their not talking about also. Mount Etna is still in the process of erupting and they said it was doing that about ten days ago. But I haven't been hearing anything about it. This is the picture again of Mount Etna in the state of erupting at the present time. If you remember both in Nastrada-

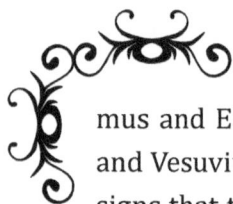

mus and Edgar Cayce the thought was when there was action on Etna and Vesuvius and it continued for a lengthn of time, these were warning signs that the pressure was building up within the earth and the earthquake level was possibly beginning to happen.

Many things are happeing with our weather, many things are happeing with our so called orbiting satellite, with the martian probe. We are hearing all kinds of fascinating kinds of ideas coming about now because it's the time that were supposed to hear these kind of fascinating ideas simply because it is the age of aquarius. As we have covered in the last two sessions, a lot is going to be happening now through the millennia both good and bad. But it is a time of change. A sign of aqaurius in astrology is a sign of mental awakening and change. Things will be revealed and concepts will come out that weren't there before. To start this particular phase part 3, the ancient history of the inner earth, I want to give you a background check and the background will simply be that our particular cosmos as it is simply called is supposedly ninety eight billion years old.

Now that might be much of an under estimate. But when you are talking about many billion years, you say one billion to me it might as well be ninety eight billion years again. Supposedly some twenty four billion years ago, there was a war in this particular galaxy. The trilogy of star wars is based on that same thing with Luke Skywalker and Darth vater. That is supposedly is based on a set of sumerain text that is true stating that some twenty four billion years ago there was a war when a whole galactic army of people fought another galactic army of people. Its been called in many cases the wars of the lord, which is one of the missing books of the ancient Hebrew text made into our bible. Its also very interesting that this also this then speaks of very advanced beings in our galaxy and later on in our solar system which have had a wonderful or terrible effect, whichever way you look at it on what has happened to our own planet earth. Let me say also this.

That our earth has gone by many names. And some of the bibles that we don't read. In the Buddhist bible, in the popuvo, and many of the oth-

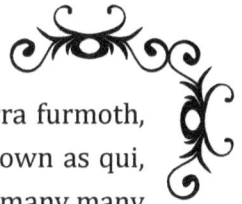

er literatures in metaphysics it has been know as terra, terra furmoth, means furmoth , its been known as tia monte , its been known as qui, its been known as shawn, as gaya, g ceros, telos, and maybe many many more it depends upon the books. I have brought with me today many of the books.Ok the paladian agenda is a book, the only planet of choice is another book, when time begans, zacahria sitchen , the seven books is another one, one that you don't even try to get, the hidden world, another book two of the hidden world,subtareanean worlds inside the earth., abc of wicca craft, secret of the ages, earth the paladian living library, zacahria yorks again , one of his scrolls and of course the one that started off the hidden world, two stories of the shaver mysteries. See I have done a lot of research ok.

You can't get some of these books. Don't even try. But I am showing you that I am not faking it. The books are there. I have read them and again to put this story together it should be very interesting. There is another part of the hidden world. None of these books you could probably get called the hidden world, but I am giving you the overview of the story as I can best put it together through all these brilliant minds and through the little exposure I had with my little contact I had I told you in 1960 and with what is happening today. And the story simply seems to go like this. That about 24 billion years ago, a people that we will simply call the els, that's els. They say that there is a whole list if you go through the encyclopedia, dictionary of el words. El elders but we will call them the els. They were called the els becasuse they were light benders. They were able to bend light therefore they were able to transverse time and what they will now call infold time. We won't spend a lot of time with that, because next week we can. Im sorry my blackboard was down.

If you can kind of see what Im putting here, we will call it first of all, the els and they were lightbenders. It meant that they could take a beam of light and they could bend it at an acute 90 degree angle. So if you say that they were able to come from what is called the four corners of earth or the four corners of time, say that one of them came from one angle, an-

other of their race came from another angle, another of their race came from another angle, and another of their race came from another angle. We get what is simply called now the cross or the bending of angles. Four ninety degree angles.

If you also will note this, if you take all four ninety degree angles and you say that this is the direction that one came from, this is the direction another came from and, this is the direction another came from and, this is the direction another came from and you put that into a flag you have the British flag. Well of course you have Stonehenge and artenbury square and many things along this line. There are also you have what is called the iron cross of hittler and the third Reich. Also if you would take one of the sacred symbols that they found in the caves, that they found down in Tiawinaco, that they found in Meroe, Yeaodo, and Africa, that they found in Madagascar Island, and it supposedly was a symbol that we use in Christainity, you get of course the cross. But if you give direction to the cross you get the swastika.

The cross which given direction shows cross man, cross minds, and cross linkage. These symbols are very interesting because they can explain to you what has happened on a planet. And they say a picture is worth a thousand words. I don't know how many words it is but you can began to see if the cross came into the swastika or the iron cross of course shows light benders then we need to understand the symbols of things and that's what hieroglyphics are all about. Heiroglyphics are said to be sacred writings that have been found throughout our planet. Petroglyphs or Petroglyphics are said to be rock wiritings. Which means again that some intelligent forms of life made these kinds of things, but the legends and the meanings are now left for interpretation. And sometimes Im afraid that that interpretation may not be correct. Lets go on with this story.

After this twenty four billion years old war our planet earth was formed through a lot of catastrophes. We will be talking about that next week. But it meant that planet preparers these people called els came into this part of system, where a solar system was being created and they

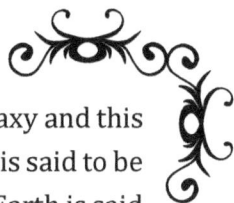

came to a very unique planet. The one planet in all of this galaxy and this solar sytem that had been worth fighting over. Because earth is said to be a man made planet, not a natural made planet. I repeat that. Earth is said to be a man made planet. Or lets put it another way rather than saying man. Its supposed to be a structure and it was created very intresetingly enough. It was imposed upon something that the creator had made and then they began to form and do more things with it. This is why on this planet you will find all kind of species of everything. And you will find all kind of insects and you find seven kinds of races.

I know you cant find five, I said there is seven. We are going to introduce two today. And of these seven different kind of races their here specifically because this planet is one of choice. And remebere I showed you this little book there. The only planet of choice. There is a book that's just called that , so let me give deference to the writer of that book. The story goes that thes els again came here to prepare this planet for a certain type of life form. Lets just say that they serve the creator and anytime a galaxy was formed and a solar system was formed and a new sun was formed they began to see what kind of life was seated upon it. Especially life that they wanted to have a specific goal in. the seated life here was very interesting because as they came to prepare this planet to show you that even the Gods and this is the only thing I can call them. I am not talking about the creator. I am talking about advanced scientific people from other planets, form other galaxies and so. So when they came here they can even goof.

And that's the best word I can think of it. They misjudged the calibrations of a sun prominence. And our sun which was a newly formed thing began to put out more radioactivity than they were ready for. Their ships rode on what they were called galactic space time. They worked on gravitational beams, they worked on magnetic fields, they worked on what they will now call lay lines. And these ships anytime you would alter a suns activity, it would affect the magnetic lines of force which means that they had problems.

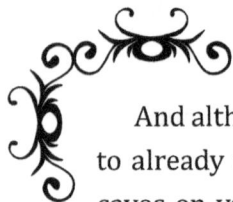

And although they were here and beginning to dig into the earth itself to already reinforce areas of our earth that was cooling by reinforcing caves on various levels. They then found out that the whole field now was due for solar prominence to come within the next twelve hours. And they had crew members if you will deep inside the earth by that time. Sometimes 1500, 2000 miles deep into the earth. They also found that our earth had another sun. And the earth had another sun by some things that we will be talking about later. But this sun was a very non radioactive sun and would be able to promulgate all types of life. But when the big sun that we now call sal, and that what a solar system is a sal system. A sal system means a sun system. And you have heard the phrase there is nothing new under a sun. Which means that this is not the first time this kind of thing has happened.

This is over what we call a time warp , where we have to seemingly learn what is going on. At any rate it goes on again. They found out that our sun put out so much radioactivity that for the type of beings they were they were not solid beings. They could take on form, but they in turn you might as well say evernescent. They were very clear beings. They were like mental beings that would pull atomic structure around them when necessary. But they were not solid mass. For them to then stay on a sun system that began to put out what exeed degenerate energy , exed would be to become solids and began to be then cursed by having to stay in a system when they were really like light benders. They were planet preparers. They could go anywhere and take on the forms they had.

So there was an emergency evacuation from our solar system, they were on our moon which was supposedly slowly being formed and they were about the business of being on a planet called Venus. And they had to evacuate the entire solar system. These were the els. And in such quick evacuation they found some of their boarding party or party members had stayed too long inside the interior. And that to extract them from the sytem at this time would have caused a solid formation and where they lived solid formations could not exist. So it was decided that they

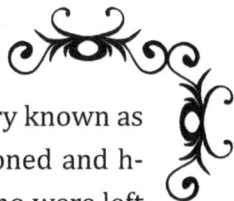

would have to be left. And they have become known in history known as the aban, the abanded ones or the abandero. That's abandoned and h- e- r – o. they have been called for short the heroes. Those who were left behind, the heroes that could not go back and be with the heavenly ones.

The fact that they fleed away from our planet and our solar system. These very advacnced light beings left a remnant here that was of their blood, that was of their crew members and so but they had erecieved too much exed energy which we now call exed energy radiation. Hwat simply had happened was our sun began to put out radiation that was only good for what they call first four levels of life. There are supposed to be thirteen levels of life.

The first four levels is now what they call a three dimensional existence and a fourth dimensional existence is what they could possibly go to. They were thirteen dimensional beings now left in a three dimensional solar system and on a three dimensional world to suffer or have whatever fate they would have. Say it again. Ok I don't know that I can say it again. There are said to be thirteen dimensions. We will go over this in our q and session if you will. I don't want to loose thought again. And that in this solar system and on this planet there are three dimensions only possible. At that time there was only three dimensions and it meant that their crew members had to take on solid form and they were now full of what they call disintegrative discs.

Disintigrative energy which caused light particles and protons to come together in form or matrix and that is supposedly what we are. We are called electromagenetic units of consciousness. Sometimes I don't know about our consciousness, but were electromagnetics and supposedly they left behind at this very interesting time millions of years ago a clue, a vestage of these people that we will call abanderos. While they had already also come from worlds without suns. That's why the statement there is nothing new under the sun came. Very vast people seemingly do not need sun systems. They don't want a sun. They have learned to create light. They are light beams themselves. When they come together light is

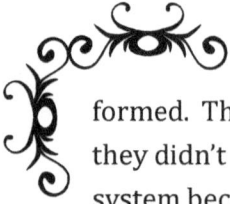

formed. They work on platonic substrata energy and plasma energy and they didn't need this kind of a system. That's why they could prepare the system because they had already graduated from some systems like this before. So you have now this analogy.

A remnant of the gods being left on a planet newly formed and living in this interior because since they did come from worlds with suns, when this sun now began to put out all this disentigrate energy they buried deeply to get away from it because it actually hurt them because they were already light beings themselves. Our sun energy was for a lower form three dimensional, three vibrational being. It was not meant for a higher degree being. So I say we start off with the a goof and if the gods can goof why cant we. At any rate with that scenario standing, then the planet earth supposedly began to cool and began to grow. That was the creators intention. And you had then within it, inside the earth there, you had there a planet as we talked about in the other two lectures that was hollow inside to a degree , with openings at its poles but had six layers of areas that could have a life with a proton energy sun and the seventh layer was a hollow. So this has openings at the poles, this has six layers going all the way around the earth like an onion, where you would have cavern worlds, large tunnels, now I already told you how large these tunnels can be, huge carverns where cities could be built.

And of course there would be more liveable space, six times more liveable space on the inside than there would be on the outside. Because on the outside you only go around once. Here you have six levels and then a liveable space with another sun interior. This is a metaphysical look at how our planet girth is supposed to be. Way out I know. But I am sure some of you have heard this before. And Ill guarantee you will hear about this more and more and more about this because it is probably the only way out. Now lets go from here and begin with that kind of a consciousness. And lets see if we can move on. These abanderos began to pick up more and more disintegrative energy or radiation and they became more and more solid based on the matrix of the planet.

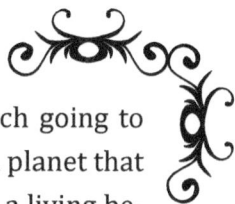

It simply means like forms on the planet are pretty much going to follow what the planet's mind is putting out. Im saying that a planet that is naturally formed is a unit of consciousness and a planet is a living being. But then there are also roys and astroids and things that are made or sometimesthere are little planets that are made in semblance of this one. This particular planet we have supposedly here is a natural planet but it has been augmented. It has already been warped. This is why it was also placed so that we would have seasons, so that we would have more than one life form capable and if you just take one shovel full of dirt, if you dare to do so, and put it underneath an electron microscope you will see its teeming with life. That's just a shovel full from any backyard you want to go to. Forms that you never think existed. Every kind of form you can think was capable of life on this particular planet, because the energies were such that this type of thing could exist.

Lets move on now with this kind of concept. These beings in their natural state were formless. They were mind workers. They could project into and form matrices of protons and molecules around them to become what they wanted to. But they were doomed to become more and more solid once they had been exposed to radiation. Supposedly radiation is your key to aging. All of the cells of our body are light bodies. Each cell has a nucleus and it has a brain in that cell. And that cell although now its been called specified cells doing specified work. The cells themselves are all constructed the same. There is a brain governor which they call a proton, there is your outer wall where they have cytoplasm again, and within the cell nucleus what protoclasm. All of them do one thing, they have in common whether they are plant cells or not they take in energy from some source and proliferate.

What does a plant do in a plant cell through photosynthesis. It takes in light and converts it to energy. So these beings were being exposed now through a very high form of radiation. And it was making them solid. They began to form solid matter and began to form bodies. Something that they would visit or make as they want to, but never did they consid-

er themselves solids. Its almost like you look at deep space nine. Now the solids versus this one particular person that can change the changelings if you look at that deep space nine series again. They have the same thing going on here. As these people begin to disintegrate it was decided by what they call a galactic council that since it was not their fault but yet they now had to go along with what this planet had to bring.

And they said maybe this is the creators will. They still said they should be given something special since it was not their fault. And although they couldn't interfere what was going to happen there, they least thought that they could get assistance. And so they sent a volunteer and a person who had a lot of wisdom by the name of Saythontis. And Saythontis was made to reincarnate as a baby. This was an old developed mind but was made to come into this planetary as a child and then was sent in a time capsule. It sounds like superman now. Into the exact area of the earth and embedded himself through this time capsule again on the third layer so that he would be between three and a half, three and a half in and three and a half out. Meaning again, the third layer in from the surface was where this time caspsule was put into a huge city or a huge cave down there and the person's name was Saythontis. That name is usually been shortened now to become Seth and you heard that name used many many times.

Seth was given the idea that he would actually become formed rather than formless and rather than being a god with no form, he was now to have a body. And the body was given a special gift as they called from the gods to be able to go to the surface for later on evolving creatures or to stay within and take control of these deroes or these abandon ones so that they would not disagree or get interface again with the natural evolving creation that the creator was going to make. The gift that they were given was melanin. Melanin was given so that it was a substance found in all of space where worlds do not have suns. Melanin is capable then of chemically adjusting to thirteen different kinds of vibrations from any sun and adjusting to that life form or that mind form where it was.

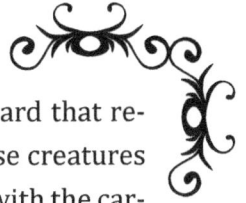

The gift of the gods was to be turned black. Now you heard that repeated different form and misused before. It meant that these creatures could now live if they were already blacked or condarkened with the carbon molecules on any planet in a solar system they could exist. And they could exist on the surface even though the life maybe short whereas any advanced being with a light body could not exist under radiation fields at all. Seth therefore became the black god of the underworld. And this is why you find so many mistranslations of Seth. Because now we have such a racial conflict that black and white and yellow and brown and red are supposed to be opposed to each other, juxta opposed. So, it's simply meant that since this life form now could live in the earth or on the earth, the adapting agent was called melanin.

Now I simply state this now not as a black man, but as a researcher. This is why to substantiatepossibly this anywhere you go on our planet earth today and you began to do research archeological, topographical, research again you will find that on any continent that you go to, the oldest citizen , the oldest person, the oldest being that you can find is a negrito. A Negrito breaks down to this. It is a short very dark to black occipital lobed pepper corned hair individual. Now that I say is any continent that you go to. By the way Europe is not a continent. We have been told that Europe is a continent. It is a peninsula. It is a peninsula of Asia. But never the less it is an island actually. No matter where you go and I repeat that the oldest person that you will find when you do research on any of the archeological digs or wherever again will be a little black dwarf simply called a negrito. I did not say negro, I did not say anything like that I said a negrito.

And this is what you will find, a small person because these creatures were first very small when they came out of the inner world that was capable of living on the surface or inside the earth as earth was formed. Again understand we are using the term earth, but I already told you there are many names for this planet. I don't want to get hung up on semantics. Also what happens after this is that with Seth there he found

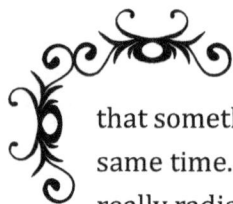

that something began to happen even worse down there and good at the same time. That this abandero had formed two units and those that got really radiated were beginning to shrivel up and become a creature that was even cannibalistic, eating themselves and eating anything that was crawling on the planet at all. Your getting a picture of what the first deroe supposedly looked like. This has been called by many the devil or Satan's emps or those that lived inside the earth that were horrid. The other form of this creature which was not at this time was not degenerated, did not get much radiation or was able to fight it off again were called teroes. Deroes were supposedly degenerate robotized individuals. Teroes were more emorphisized.

They were people who were still kept consciousness and had of course the t force which was part of which is called the cross the towel force within them. They still had life force to make them sensible, to make them not degenerate any further. And they had formed two seperate socities within the earth. If you remember H.D. Wells had the same thing with the morlocks. There is always retrospect to this in many cases. But I say we will move on as we are doing now. Now an evolving life form began to form on the planet itself. These were the creatures that we now call apes or apu if you would. Another life form that was winged began to form on the earth. Many fish began to form in the oceans of earth.

And because of this war that had been fought some24 billion years ago, two of theplanets in our system was able to now send this life form to this planet and because of karma which means jsutificantion for actions done they had to reincarnate on our earth now because they caused the moon of earth to be formed. So now you have people coming to earth from two other planets and evolving life form from the creator and the blood line of the gods deep within the earth all sharing the same planets. Now were going to go back now, I want to do, to take a look at another side of things, which is to take a look at another side of things. 12,960 years ago there was a reawakening that happened on our planet. And of course we are going to refer to it from this time on as earyh again. A

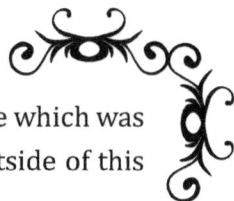

people that have been called the nocke men, the nocke people which was short for the ananocke from the planet neberu, which is outside of this particular constellation.

They came here for certain reasons. We will talk about that next week. They came here and they wanted to utilize what was going on on this planet and in fact they found the whole solar system and especially earth very enjoyable. It was a galactic meeting what is called the galactic federation in which they were said they could do some things but it was decreed that there would be three other systems that would have a lot to do with what happened on earth. One was called Sirius. And we had the Syrians come in from the planet Sirius. The other again was called the paladians, including a very negative star solar system called Orion and also the people from which is called neberu. All of these it was agreed would have an important part to play on what happened on our planet. They agreed to this alliance began because it was stated that the earth and the solar system would soon be going into what was called a photon band.

Not a belt, but a photon band. And so Neberuains were given the right to choose a culture that they could enter into by incarnation. They choose the Fertile Crescent even though they really wanted kemet. Kemet was Africa but they chose to come down to the area now at the Fertile Crescent. Where we are having these big wars. We always talk about Iraq, Iran. All of those areas and what was called mespotamia 1. The syrains were allowed to continue to keep developing Africa itself or at that time it was called Kemet. Since their ancestors had already made contacts and they built the sphinx roughly around 18000 B.C. 17800B.C It was the syrians who built the sphinx. The sphinx and the pyramid were not built at the same time. The paladians were given again the ability to continue teaching earth's people as it was said that they also were developed by these els. And so the els gave them the contract if you would to work with earth developing species again. But the right to incarnate was taken away from the paladians. They had to do it by mind control. The right to maintain coz or souls that could enter into a person or into some of the bodies developed that was taken away.

They either of had to been flesh born or what they call sweat born or they had to influence mentally because there were a very advanced system and it was felt that there would not be gratification enough for them to do so. So three different units of consciousness were assigned to workers, the niberians, the syrains, and the paladians. Each one having their own vestiage, each one finding out what they wanted to do. Now one of the reasons for the counsel that decided that is why I want to. The solar system came out of the photon belt. At the end of the age of Leo, which was 8640 B.C. and the high waters that were there flooding everywhere began to recede.

The world was a different place again and began what is called the fourth grade cycle. Prior to that it was decided again that the great flood and the entrance to the photon belt was going to effect everything on the earth again.Before the gods left in 14200 B.C. they showed how to listen to the sounds of the galaxy by drums, rattling, and balls in swamps with amphibians, insects, reptiles, and birds. The paladian shamans were very challenged by this new teaching because it got them in touch with other stars and all of you realize that their were other stars influencing the earth besides the paladians. When the ananocke gods went away to some every far off place in the sky, you watched the paladian body leave and then the sky was study hoping that they would return and bring back to you life that you began to understand.

At 13364 to 8239 B.C., a change really began to happenon earth when the solar system is in the photon belt. The sky gods and shamans had talked about the special nature of this particular place and how to make stone temples to enhance energy so that you could work with guardian spirits. Large groups of affiliated clans began to identify with one place or another. These special qualities of these began to imprint you and its called differeniateyou according to higher regional you zones you became the people of the canyon, the lake, the higher plateaus, or Great

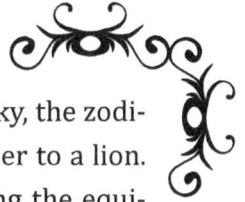

Mountain. Certain places were aligned with animals of the sky, the zodiac. One place was special to a wolf, another to a bear, another to a lion. More and more people prayed at these special places during the equinoxes and solstaces as light beams began to shift from the inner sun. You discover the inner world and the animal's star teachers. These animal guides could feel whirlwinds spinning out of turluric zones and they could see these spirals traveling out in the night sky to the stars. 11000 B.C. in alliance was made between the paladians, syrains, and nubians, because all three groups knew that the solar system was approaching the photon band.

The syrians are able to incarnate the clan only when earth vortexes are activiated by the guardians of sacred places and the animals could begin to resonate with the stars. A great awskening of gatian revolution was accomplished during the evolution of Virgo 12960 – 10800 B.C. that is similar to the awakening that you feel at the end of the age of Pisces and will soon feel at the end of the Age of Aquarius. Im going to go from that to simply say that while this was going on we still have these higher form beings living inside the earth being now part and partial of what was happening on the outside of the earth. And they began to form their own societies, because they felt that they were better than the evolving life forms. And then it was these other planets began to form their own mutations if you would.

They had what they call synthetics, they had clones, they had cross breeds, and they began to form a great society that was called lamooria on the surface of the earth. Now we have covered that in one of our other lectures. Now just a overgo of that. La moooria was in the Pacific Ocean. A huge continent on which everything west of the Rocky Mountains, in our own United States it was part of. It was an ingraft station from lamooria that formed what is California, Orgeon and all these places. That's why things there were better, bigger, and looked different from the rest of the area that is now what we call the United States of America. This particular continent also had some battles that were fought with

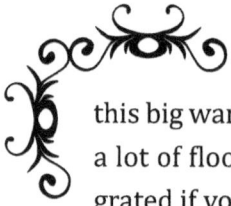

this big war. Well talk about that next week. This galactic war that caused a lot of flooding and things in two of our planets systems to be disentigrated if you would.

So you had now all of this chaos going on on the surface and all of this change. While inside still live these very advanced beings, degenerate now in form split up into two different societies. These societies that the paladians began to work with produced a being by the name of Lilith. That's l – i-l – i- t- h or said to be the witch of the caves if you would. Lilith has been referred to in many of the books and so as the moon goddess. She has been referred to as the femme fatale. Referred to as the enticing sorceress, the beautiful vampire with a loving inhuman type of disposition that caused everyone to flock to her. She had one big flaw.

She had great claws on her feet like that of a bird. And this is why you will find depicted whenever you see the term Lilith a beautiful woman with claws. This is said to be one of the transfixings, one of the creatures that was made to govern certain people on this surface of earth. But also was given the privelage of contacting people on the moon and people inside our earth itself. Im going to read to you a little bit about Lilith again. She is depicted in this way on a terracotta relief in Sumner that means ancient mespotamia again dating about 2000 B.C. the same figure of hermetaphres dreams recurred in medieval France where she was known as la femme fatale.

The queens with the birds foot a mysterious figure of legend who flew by night at the head of a crowd of phantoms something like the wild hunt. The Jewish legends about Lilith say that, she was the first wife of Adam, before eve was given to him. Lilith however came to Adam as he lay asleep and coupled with him in his dreams. This means she became the mother of all uncanny beings that stirred this planet invisibly with mortals that are known as the ferry races of the gin. The Jews regarded her as queen of the evil spirits and made amulets to protect themselves and even summoned her to help fight against mortal people. She is the personification of erotic dreams that troubles mens suppressed desire

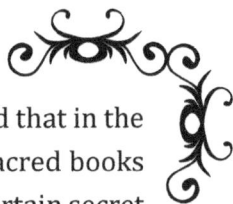

for forbidden delights. Now keeping that in mind, understand that in the Jewish religion, in the michnatorah and some of the more sacred books they talk about and honor Lilith. As we live today there are certain secret societies that still pray to Lilith to come and help.

She is said to be the mother behind the mother. And if we are taking this whole thing to be true, then she is the person who supposedly drains men dry. She is supposedly the person who can live in heaven, on the earth, or inside the earth itself.And she becomes the mother adjacent to eve. She is a certain person who is believed in by many of or two of the races of man and one of the great religions of man in what is now called the Jewish concept. There is a whole story about Lilith,. But that is the way that is most pure. You can began to interpret it as you would. But it is said that she spawned a differnet people, served a different people, and was not meant to serve all the races of man. But she was Lilith for those who understood her.

Another one of the names that you will find in history that must be gotten into to make sense of the underworld is what is also called the power of three hecatec.I pronounce it hecata.Notice again how I did do the pronounciation. She has the power of three. She has been referred to as the old chrome, the Hecate one. That's Hecate, the nameless one, afra-tos, pondiera, the terrible. Some say she is the anceient Greek goddess of withcraft and thrown by the Romans by having her life engraved on gems an sculptures as having three heads, three pairs of arms each one held daggers, whips, and torches, and at her feet were two huge circles.

This is how she is usually pictured I medieval times and in the Grecian Parthenon and so on and so on like this. Many scholars of classical Greek and roman culture believie her to be an extremely ancient goddess or a person who had a great affect in the surface world and the older world. Many of them say that she is older than the classical Olympians that must have been at the time when the earth was just being formed. Even though the Greeks believed she was granted the time honored power of granting or withholding form mortals whatever their hearts desired.

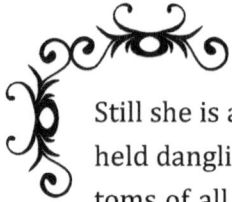

Still she is an anomaly. Another one of her symbols was a key which she held dangling from one her hands indicating her ability to release phantoms of all kind. Years ago we called her queen of the phantom world. In Shakepear's MacBeth, the witches did not worship the devil or Satan. They worshiped Hecata. And Thomas Riddleton played the witch, Hectata is said to be the chief goddesses of all the witches. She has said also her statute was the one that was shown at the crossroads.

They found that so called people of the heath, the heathens, farmers, and people who understood trolls and gobblins. Ireland and the Scotland and places again, in ancient Egypt there is what is called a crossroads. This is where paths would cross and this is where they found the ancient sites of hecata. This is where they began to build these churches believe it or not, at the crossroads. This is where the gypsies or those who feed gyps or those who feed Egypt also carried on the teachings of hecata. She is said to be a goddess, queen over Diana, atremess and selene. The goddesses of the moon if you would. So therefore her power was in the heavens of earth and on the earth itself and even in the underworld. She has again according to the stories, the circle or the crescent moon and a star where everything was in Greek. It showed an inverted cresecent moon for hecata and then another prong was put so it becomes like partial of the trident.

One of the symbols of hecata used for what is called the crafts of the wise. There was a battle that was fought between hecata and Saythontis as she began to represent one of the paladian goddesses. As he represented what was called now the anonocke or the els. It was stated that they both wanted domination of the earth itself form the inner to the outer. This led to what was called a large change for the people on the surface of earth that were governed by these people on the surface of earth by these so called gods or these so called personages and it led to a lot of the racial wars that we now undergo. Because at one time understand that none of these people here had forms. Especially the highest one and then as races were developed on the earth, each one belonged to

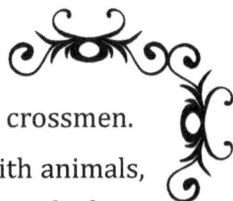

a different system of gods. And you also had what was called crossmen.

You had people that were then crossed by the anoncke with animals, making them animal people. In addition to some that were brought from outer space, like you now have the Asiatics. And if you remember the Japanese state that their supposed to run this earth. The Germans said that they were supposed to run this earth. They wanted to rule the world. And if you notice on the Japense flag it states that they are of the seveneth grade. Youll notice that they have the rising sun and they state again that they were not born of earth and are not supposed to be of earth. And that's one of the reason there has been a battle for the dominance of the Japenese. They even fought the Chinese who said they were from the earth and were not as golden or not as yellow as they were. All of these things you will find in the history books.

I am only giving you now teas that you will make you possibly understand what has gone on here or what has possibly gone wrong here. Inside the earth as they began to build up these kingdoms and some of the people from neberu and some of the people from Syria and from the Palades again they began to form colonies also inside the earth. And when they came to vist the earth to see what was going on, they didn't land onto the surface they came into the polar orfices.

And then they would send out their, if you want to call it their scientists to visit the various people and they would sometimes come out of caves themselves. Sometimes they would come out of the caves in what were called ventalas. These were earth flying spaceships riding on anti gravity beams that would float out. They could not go into space. But they would go to these big motherships inside the earth. But when they came out of the earth they were on these things called ventalas. You will hear of the term called ventla it was used a lot. This was the things, the chariots of gods that flew around visiting the various sites.

They were like no fly zones or areas that the paladians told the syrains don't go there. There were places where the neberians told the other people not to go there. But a people from the Plaetes called the Orinians

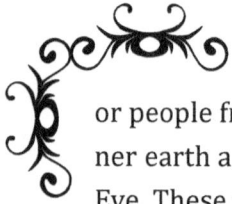

or people from Orian defied those laws, came in, and pulled from the inner earth a group of people which later on became known as Adam and Eve. These were the people again that were sent there set aside by only the Syrains to be developing into a new concsciousness. But again these peole came there and told them well they shouldn't go through this, they had as much rights as anybody else on the planet. And you began to see how a lot of these problems began to be played if you would.

There are a lot of stories too about gravity and gravity having changed. Age comes on the planet earth because of radiation. Radiation comes on the planet earth because of the inability to cells to adjust to varying frequencies. This came about because this planet was not for just anybody that did not have melanin or later on developed that way. Melanin gives you the privelage of adjusting to different ferquencies. But melanin will do one thing. It will make the body when it forms a matrix dark because the worlds that are in space that do not have vibrational frequency can be adjusted. So the gift of the gods was for any of these people to be able to live on any of the planets in our sytem inside or outside. Because of this they were able to with the help of what is called anoncke to begin to develop the kind of consciousness that allowed them to build and move great stones.

That allowed them to understand the history of the earth itself and begin to also put them in conscious disntinct level with the other people that have been brought in by the paladians and the other people that have come from Orion and so on and so on like this. So you have now conflict if you will.Based even on all that it is now exacerbated because then you have people in mu and they don't want a colony of mu atlantis now beginning to cross genes to cross insect genes, to cross winged reptile genes, to cross amphibian genes, and began to make people which they released in the earth but only to the area of the fertile crescent. These cross linkings or these cross people then began to rebel against that and began to go any where they want to and began to war with humans.

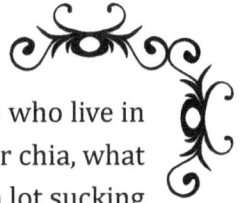

That's where you hear the story of velcaroris. The people who live in the cave and came out and even now where your getting your chia, what do you call it this person that you hear on the art bell show a lot sucking people dry. Can't even think of the name of it now, chupacabra. They are not new either becasuse to have many of these vampire like creatures that were cross breed that also resented what went on and felt that they should have a position to say on earth. Earth is a very interesting place as you can began to see. The point was it was never told how these things all got started. That each one was supposed to stay in a certain era until which time everybody could grow in light.And also keep in mind too the metaphysics statement that everything that has life and is capable of holding thought will be given a planet to develop to its highest potential. This one took on a lot, not only did it have seven different races but even in sectoids and humanoids and drones and cross breeds and everything else. It is a planet of choice and it is a mess.

To now state to live on the planet earth at a time again when it is going to go through a photon belt and at a time when consciousness is supposed to revive up because our sun is again now putting out more energy, more magnetic energy, and to get tripple promoted.Any person that can say that they had a so journ on this planet earth and came out sane is supposedly rewarded. That's the best way I can give you as an overview. I know it sounds very way out because it is very way out. And for specific details if you like Im going to turn it over to questions and comments for you to get more so into this planet, bf, earth, Shawn, tellos, terra, nibiru, no not niberu, but qwe and all of the various names it has. It has many, all of our continents are now misnamed or they have changed names.

So when you go back in history it becomes very difficult because the names that we now use were not used then. In fact at one time people didn't even have a language. They spoke with mind thought, because they were formless.

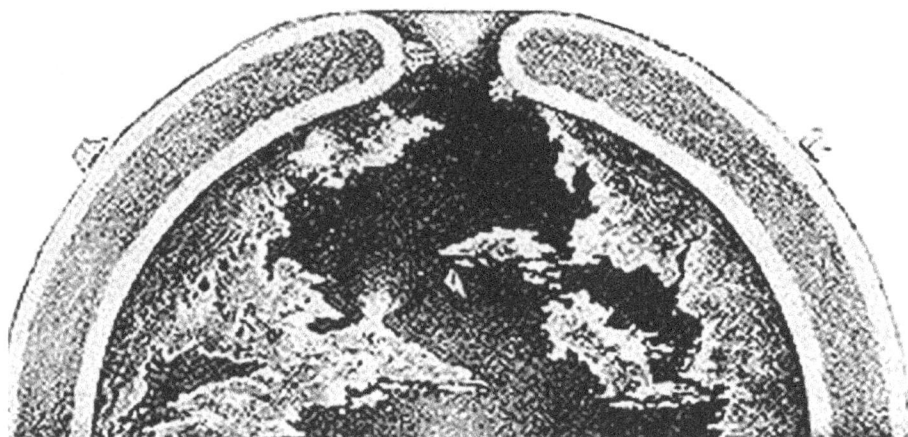

The World Within
Part 4-1

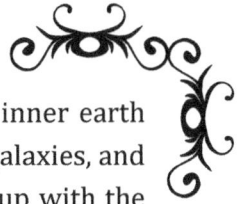

*T*he lecture is the world within series, part 4, inner earth and people from the interior of other plants, galaxies, and moons. It required a lot of research to come up with the conlcusions I have reached today. And to present to you the various assumptive and pragmatic ideas that are going to be conveyed. A lot of research and I like to give honor and credit to people whose books I have used and whose knowledge I have perked as well as to research of course its not in book form. One book very hard to get is the Sky People, another Invisible Residence, another ManKind Child of the Stars, another the Prism of Lyra, another Your Becoming a Galactic Human, and many other books Dr. George Bernard Hollow Earth, George Hunt Williamson Roll in the Sky.

And as I say this was a culmination of about thirty years research to present what I am giving you today. I will say as I do in all of my lectures there is no truth until you decide what truth is. I repeat there is no truth until you decide what truth is. It does not mean that there is no truth but it means that we are all products of our truths. We live our life according to what we think is right. And consequently whatever I am saying to you, if you doubt it, do your own research. All Im trying to do is give you a format by which at least you can find some truth. But by all means find some kind of truth soon. I think it's really necessary. We're going to talk about a journey now that we are going to take. And as they say in the movie star wars to a galaxy far far away. I kind of challenge and say that Speilberg's movie star wars is based on a number of books and on something that happened in our galaxy that is very true. The point is they will never tell you where they originated from.

They just tell you a galaxy far far away. Were going to take a trip now to over four million years ago. As we register earth time and in the Palladian galaxy in the constellation of Orion on a planet known as tyrantor, a number of inhabitants two different kinds of people. They call themselves tyres, sometimes tyrants, because they were people of tyrantor a planet in the Orion console and the Orion galaxy. This was a very large

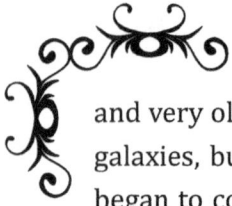

and very old intelligent race of people. And they populated a number of galaxies, but their central planet was called tyrantor. On tyrantor they began to come up with what they call computerization. And they perfected computers to such a point that even robots and everything else was done through the use of computers. Sound kind of familiar.

They got so specific with these computers that they created what they call a robot species with synthetic skin and computer chips. They were able to do everything manually by somebody else's effort. They had a lot of time to think they had a lot of time to create, a lot of time to recreate, and they lived for almost a thousand some years. And then usually they caused their death or caused what you call their transition on their own. It was a very very modern planet if you would began to think about what we call modern appliances.And every convenice you can think of now, can imagine they had. They made one mistake. They put a group of seven people which they were called tyrantors or tyres in charge of the planet tyrantor. And they began to have so many computers and so many large thinking machines on this planet that they began to do the work for all of their solar system.

There were twelve planets in the solar system. And everybody in the solar system combined together to follow the tyrants lead. The tyrantors and the people, the scientists who worked these computers. The scientists decided at one time, that they had a very powerful position. They found that whatever they stated that people would do, because the machines calculated the weather, they controlled their weather, the machines calculated death,they controlled death, the machines calculated organ replacements,they controlled their organ replacements, the machine did all the things for the home, had beautiful forests and everything was done by machines and computerized. The people simply grew somehat lazy, very strong, very intelligent, and a bask again in the luxury of having everything being done for them.

Then it hit them again, these men the item called greed. They began to say well with this kind of power and since nobody challenges us and since nobody doubts us, we can pretty much make these programs any-

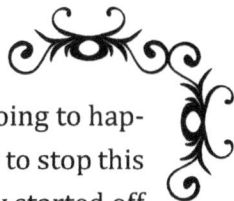

thing we wanted to. We could tell the people anything was going to happen and they would believe it. We say we make the computer to stop this from happening, to protect them from it. To encapsulate they started off with those twelve planets in that system. And they went on until finally they had some thirty other planets that were all part of now what they call the tyrant confederation. Then they began to find as they went further and further out that some of the people on the more distant galaxies and more distant stars began to doubt them and say well I don't know if we want to have this.

This is kind of exercising and taking control away from us.And they began to fight wars and began to threaten. And they got so powerful with these weapons and the kind of machines that they use that everybody began to knuckle under what they call the tyrant galaxy or the tyrantors. It went on till they had 106 solar systems under their command. And then they said we should go out and start wars with other constellations wherever we can find life because we are dominant and we are supreme. Well at that time then they began to build a confederation of people who upholds this kind of thought. And these people came together much as in star wars to oppose this dark star which was called dyrantor, which is nothing now but a big computer.

And all of the things they were doing because they said it was unspiritual and unsoullike and it was making a mockery out of intelligent life and out of spiritual life. So they began to fight this war for close to half a million years. It went on through generation after generation. And it involved many others of the solar systems and many other galaxies and constellations. And then finally the confederation that opposed them was so strong that they began to beat them back so they finally got into what they would call six solar systems. Which has come to be known in metaphysical and illumanati circles as the unholy six. Six solar systems with twelve planets each which refused to have peace, which refused to knuckle under any kind of spiritual vibration and stated that we like the way things are and so whether to anhilate them they quaranteened them.

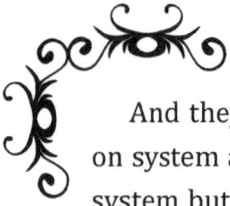

And they left what is called the unholy six and that part of the Orion system and they caused them to not be able to travel past the Orion system but to have to stay within it. But they had perfected again telecommunication. They had perfected again transcription using thought waves,and even though they were allowed or made to stay physically within those six solar sytems in the orion and plaetes they could then project their thoughts and they used what they called tellav projection to reach neighboring systems and whenever there were certain planets in a system where experimental life and soul life was needed to progress they began to affect them because its been said that in every universe and in very constellation there are at least twenty two planets that are set aside for wayward souls, for people who have to learn the hard way, for souls again who need to be perfected or need to be strong. And those souls then go untouched.

Whatever migrates there, whatever incarnates there is said to be going through a phase of training. Such a system of course is one that we now live on. But before we get into where we live, let's go with the conclusion of what happened supposedly there in Orion on this planet tyrantor. The people who the scientists who we wont call mad, but very coventous, very greedy, very wanting to be worshiped and all like this, began to argue among themselves and finally they brought about the destruction of tyrantor because they sought to launch a beam type weapon using both mind and solar control. Which they thought if they could sneak and get it off they could began to destroy many of the key planets and they also thought to take over some of the key leaders in the confederation.

And their plan failed and the beam that they sent out returned, came back and hurling toward them and they were wiped out. They were anhilated if you would. But even though they were anhilated they still maintained a number of robots that had been placed on various orbiting satellites.Some of which were not known by the confederation, which were prrogramed to continue to send out these teleopathic signals to

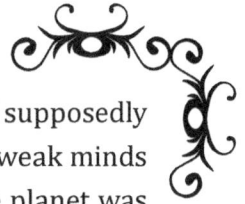

reach any souls that were weak enough to be conformed.And supposedly until very recently they broadcast this on a regular basis to weak minds to weak souls, and other galaxies, and other places. But the planet was called tyrantor where we get the word tyrant.

The people on it, tyres or tyrants. And it s because they were tryants that we got our word tyre or tyrants. If you notice again now there is a word called tyranasuarus. There is a lot of words that use the same word tyre. These were creatures that were aslo spawned by computers in that system and were isolated to that system at one time because they were nothing but killers. Tyranasaurus rex was one of the chief killing machines almost like the shark, the killing machine of the sea. These are not natural to planets. These are things that were made in laboratories by these people who not only could gene splice and clone but they could also subjugate phylums. They could cross phylums if you would. Keeping that story in abeyance, we are going to move to another story equally as way out. But supposeldly all true when we study metaphysical literature if you would. This is only approximately 70,000 years ago and there was a planet in the orbit that now sits inbetween mars and Jupiter. The planet was called maldeck. This maldecian planet in a solar system like all solar systems is comprised of twelve planets. We have been told we have nine.

All solar systems have twelve planets, which means that there are three planets that we know nothing about. At this particular one it was very interesting because for some things that they did they became the thirteenth planet. The thirteenth planet was known as maldeck and it had an orbiting moon which was known as malona. Maldeck and malona between the orbit of Jupiter and mars. Some systems say that it was called fullaria and others say it was called saytania. Saytania, fullaria, or maldeck's or its moon malona, depends on whose story your hearing and what time it is being related. We are talking about the same thing, a planet orbiting between the orbits of Jupiter and Saturn again. Approximately seventy thousand years ago, the people there began to develop fusion as well as fissional material. They atomic fusion, the had atomic fission.

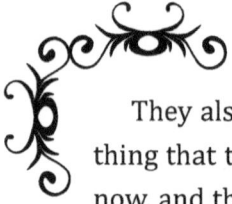

They also used this to began to transform molecules, to do the same thing that they did in tyrantor although this was way across the galaxy now, and they began to make life now, they began to infuse and confuse as I like to say. And most of the words we use are based again on a different kind of understanding. Confusion, subtrafused, fusion whichever again. It only means to con the mind and take away from the understanding that we are all one. That ther is a universal creator and a universal power and that the whole idea is to understand that and begin to respect that power. They would began to make what we now call atomic weapons. They even went into hydrogen fusion. And it's even worse than fission because it first implodes before it explodes.

And two factions were there. One had taken up vestiges on their moon malona and they had a secret project by which they were going to use this material to focus down on one of their continents and destroy the people, hold the planet as hostage , and take over much as what they had done in another system which we call tyrantor. These people there plotted to destroy a certain section of the planet more or less as a scape goat more or less as an example. At the same time the other ones found out they were going to do this and they planned on destroying a portion of their moon. And it so coincided that within the same twenty four hour period they set aside these beam weapons and a fusion and fission material to do what was done. It started a chain reaction of hydrogen material and lead to the complete anhilation of both Maldeck and Malona. Since at that particular time it had taken up refuge in a system that already had twelve planets, and this calls for another story, it was called the thirteenth planet or the unlucky planet from what we get what is called now triscodecaphobia. It is the fear of the number thirteen.

Because when that thirteenth planet blew itself up and had to be replaced it set off a chain reaction in our solar system that is still going on. It caused havoc among the smaller planets and chaos among the larger planets. The two planets that have suffered the most were Jupiter and of course mars because they were on either side of them. And in the case

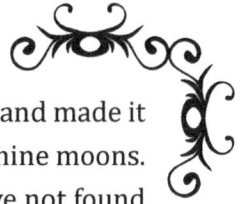

of Jupiter it split up many of the fragments of their big moon and made it into little moonlets. This is why Jupiter now supposedly has nine moons. We understand it to be twelve moon, three of those they have not found yet. But then it aslo created havoc on mars. Mars once it blew up had its top sheared off by a portion of the maldecian planet. It had all the water to be absorbed and it almost sent out into space including the water that was also vaporized on malona cuz it had a lot of water there.

So it had that that wasn't vaporized now combining as a big flood of water coming through our solar system from mars, maldeck, and malona. The planet earth which has many names and we have talked about that before , well just call it earth for now received a deuage of this material. And this is one of the many floods and there have been seven floods that happened to this planet. This was the most devastating and it aslo brought to our planet salt water which had never berfore been on the planet earth. Which there was nothing but freshwater.

The gorges and craters were filled up and they became oceans. And whole land masses were changed. And not only did you have freshwater on the planet earth, but now saltwater from mars, saltwater from maldeck, and saltwater from malona radioactive in many cases. It brought with them the incumbancy and the incubation period of different species of fish and mamalians that could never live on this planet before. But now thrived in little embryonic eggs that also came through space after this planet destroyed itself. The marshians were a very advanced race of people at this particular time. They lived on a surface because they had melanin. Every planet that has surface dwellers must have melanin to adapt. And if you go back again to understand the story we told last week again it shows that melanin is your key feature if you are going to live on the surface of a planet. Other than that intelligent life forms live inside a planet protected from radiation, protected from the sun, from the moon, and from intergalactic space.

Because rays, exed rays, and cosmic rays are always bombarding and they change life forms. They change the life that we now understand.

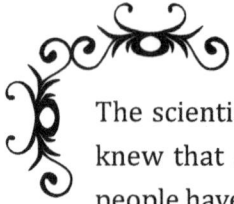

The scientists on mars which was also called massa, decided that they knew that something was going to happen on maldeck because these people have been more or less waring and they began to pick up through their teleopathic ability that something was going to happen. Many of them fled the whole system rather than this. Some who couldn't flee the system tried to do what they could at the time of trial. And when the planet finally did blow them off, they had sought to inside their planet. They went inside their own planet there in order to exist through the chaos that racked throughout the marshaian atmosphere. The water was vaporized, a big hole was cut off the top of mars, and they put up to stop the whole planet from being shunted as they call it into space. They put up two orbiting satellites what we now call moon or moonlets.

One was called Phobos. The other was called demos. Panic and fear. These moons were put up there to balance mars and stop mars from going out of orbit and they were put up amongst panic and fear both from the Maldekians as well as the Marshians themselves who didn't want to die or have their whole planet destroyed. They are both artificial satellites. Even though they are now part of the astronomy system that we now teach, both of those are metal and they are made up of other fiberous material. They are artifiacial satellites and if you remember fobos moon is in retrograde in a very fast cycle which moves against the grain. By one moving against the grain and the other one moving to the grain the planet was able to be balanced by use of what is called vortex or vortex spears.

These people that were then there on mars now had to live inside and since they now found that earth itself which was called shawn, cerros, tiamont, it has many names now was able to hold their type of life because of the various vibrational changes. And this is after the earth stabilized almost after a hundred years of turmoil after that terrible thing that happened to it. They then sent some of their people to live on this planet. And what is called the galactic elohem.Those union of those people of very high resolve and spiritual natures decided that since earth had been

so contaminated with the vibration of other planets that a mixture of people would be allowed to live on the planet earth and they could dwell wherever the planet had decided to put this new material and they could dwell according to the vibrations of the planet and according to the vibrations that they had there too. At this time I might give a break down metaphysically of what is called the creation of what we are and how things are so segmented.

There is said to be in metaphysics that there are seven universes. There are three cosmos. There are seven universes. Each universe is divided into 144 sectors or sections. Each sector is divided into 144,000 galaxies. Each galaxy further divided into 144 million constellations. Each constellation divided into twelve solar systems. Each solar system divided into twelve planets. And age is the time it takes for any of the solar systems with their suns to pass through one of what is called the signs of the constellation or zodiac. And this is called a dispensation.

It takes 2100 years to pass through one of the twelve signs in a dispensation. Again we get from that 14400 that we talk about so much. It is not so much 144000 people as it is the sections and sectors, and galaxies that all undergo change because they are all governed by suns. And each sun is linked to each other suns almost like a step down transformer. That's why its been said that there is nothing new under a sun. Because all suns send in intelligence and they support the life of planets.There are said to be in our solar system and especially in galactic worlds, worlds without suns, who don't want suns.Because they can generate their own light, their own intelligence, and their own suns. But those who need to be incubated, need the sun to protect them, a sun to cut the information again as it would be , and through this way again so are planets brought into be. As we now understand them, that lives inside the planet mars or Massa are a people who look Negroid.

Seventy percent of the population of mars is Negroid. Other than that you also have synthetics which were people that were made much like were beginning to understand it is now possible to make skin. They are

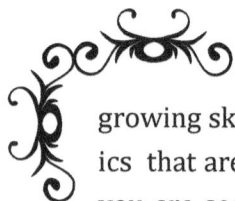

growing skin and they can make limbs now as you understand for bionics that are stronger than even the person. That is not a joke. And what you are seeing now in predator and Arnold Schwarteznagger are very realistic. You can make a creature that is half chip computer and half synthetic skin where bullets can bounce off and Robocop if you want to mesh it with silicon and metal. These things were there also. And it is a marshian gift if you would when used correctly. But they do not have souls. Im not saying that all marshians do not have souls.

These synthetic creatures that came from mars have no souls. But they look many times like the marshains themselves. And they were sent here more or less to test the atmosphere to see how much radiation had been left from the deuage that came from maldeck, and malona, and from all the other things that happened in our solar system that calls for background radiation. If you go back to the first one we presented, even the so called els, the lyrians, and the other people who were very evolved can goof. And if you remember that's how our first class on the inner world ended where they didn't even chart the sun rays on our own planet and had to leave that written inside the earth. So, again suns are very precarious things. You have to check their fields, you have to check the vortex that their within or life can be affected by a sun anytime at all. These martians then who came here have explorers,ave people who wanted to see if their planet had been so devastated they could find another planet to live on and also new to contact those who already inside the earth because they knew the earth was a wonderful place because the descendants of the els and Seth lived inside of it because of the goof what is called the elder race. That also is on the other tape so I won't go into that. When they came here they also stopped off at their own moon which was formed agian through another catstrophe that happened sometime ago.And the moon of course was know to be a spaceship.

It was known to be a non perfect satellite, one that had crashed, that still had some ancient mechanisms still capable of movement. This is why the moon had such a balanced thing around our planet. And you use

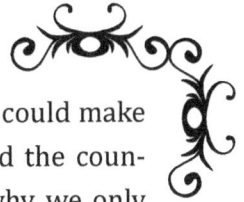

the opposite side of the moon and change the rotation, you could make the moon so one side always faced the earth as it matched the counterbalance and the resonation of the earth itself. This is why we only see one side of the moon and supposedly there is a vast civilization on the side that we do not see and they use this almost like a waste station when they are coming to the earth, contact the people in the inner earth, in agartha and shamballa and then make their ventures forth. But at the same time that the marshainas came here and used the moon they wanted to again set up theirt own colonies here they found that the same people, these degenerate people from the els who had gone through this radiation contaminaton had now began to repopulate. They had done so again by using what they call stem devices, cell bionics, and cloning. And they resented them coming to the earth itself. So rather than to start another war, as there had been turmoil already in the galaxy they called for what is called the fathers fo the light the elohem to try and see who should be dispensated to live on the earth and what control should be had there.

So certain sections were set up where these people who had been devastated by the maldeckain catastrophe could live in hopefully in peace and in harmony and could set up their own type of life forms as they so choose each one to their own sector. Again it didn't work too well. As in most cases they were all always those who are not agreeing. And even one of the elohem said agiain why should he go through this again when he has been shown that the creator can also seemingly goof because he used the example maldeck and malona, he used tyrantor, and he said again if this happens anyway who are we to say what should be right.

Maybe it is our point to become like the creator, to become as a god, and to do the things that a god should do or creator should do. And so it was decided that since he felt this way and was going to cause some more turmoil that he would be isolated to the moon only. And it was found that many people that reached to a certain development state on their planet if they felt that they could do better than to stay on the plan-

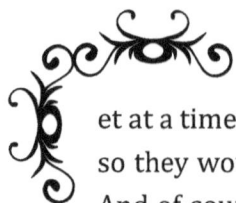

et at a time before they were allowed to go into other constellations and so they would be placed on moons. And moons always orbited planets. And of course the moons were places where they could think the thing over and not harm the type of life form that would be developing on a particular planet.

Our present society and even as we speak supposedly Monday will start sending back pictures of Sedona on Mars. Sedona on Mars and this is why this lecture is so very timely is one of the ancient marshian cities. And any time you find stone structures on our earth, on our moon, or on mars, it means that beneath there is an underground city. Many of these are used for piping areas to filter out the air. They use it agin for conveyances and to put telepathic thought out and to communictate with their own ventlas, farmanas, and avalanches.

This is what they call their ships. And it also means that once the people on this planet which are cross section of everything from a synthetic man, deroes, teroes, lyrians, Syrians, all of the things that we have talked about before began began to realize again who they are and who their gods were and more or less who helped to create them. That there would be turmoil again. This is why now the NASA, which is interesting too. That's wht it is called is hiding so much of what they have already found on Mars, on our moon, on Venus, on Isle, on Low, on Jupiter. All of these things where they have found obvious remnants of intelligent life and since they were contacted it was talked about before through the time when they first experimented with the Tesla princliples back in 1947, then they already know what is up there. In fact they have colonies on Mars already. Russia has a colony on the moon and on Mars, United States has a colony on moon and on mars, and two of the presidents were assisinated when they were told share this with the people.

The people should understand that they had different aliens in government and that there was a war going on that was imbalanced, so impetous that if anything should happen anyone of these other species might take over. This has been a problem we have had with society for a

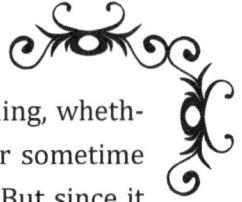

long time, whether to tell people what was actually happening, whether to take elected officials who were synthetic or cloned or sometime with no melanin and give them the power to run a planet. But since it was decided that all chaos that happened here anyway, they let the best rule whether they were soulless or whether they had souls if they developed to a point where they could become less hostile, they developed to a point where intelligence could be learned,ad they said so be it.

And the planet earth was one of choice. This is where the book came from the Only Planet of Choice, where the choice was either like you were condemned here or that you wanted to come here because you can began to show what you have learned and how powerful you could be. Our own moon has within it a hollow interior with a lot of propulsion mechanisms which could make the moon actually move. The moon was then reprogrammed by a very advanced species of people which we will talk about next week again. But what well say for now, niberains or dracons if you would to keep the earth life from becoming sistient to a strong degree. In other words they set up a radiation field which would stop the progression of cells from ever becoming like gods or ever becoming undying or ever becoming almost multiplistic in their consepts in order to have greater brain power. We have here too strong an electrical field.

The electrical field here stops things from maturing, causes death, and holds back progression. One that field was set up and its ability to do so again was of various vibrations, from mars, from maldeck, and so like that. And it broke a natural twelve strand DNA pattern and caused it now only to be two strands. It cut again the chromosome patterns and the DNA patterns so that people now could not do what they used to be able to do if they had melanin. Our genetiscists now call that junk melanin, junk DNA. There is no such thing as junk DNA. DNA which does not recombine recompitent and have 12 strands is simply DNA that has been messed with if you would be DNA that is now in confusion. And as our planets sun is now changing it will cause the moon to give off left energy. And if you notice you have had a lunar eclipse this year and a solar

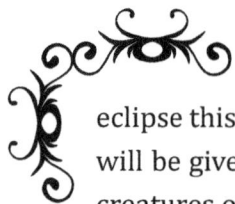

eclipse this year. That is is a sign that shows that the governship of earth will be given back to the sun and taken away from the moon. And solar creatures or solamen or a men or people who are sealed with sal.

Sun people and will now be able to reunite their DNA strands, be able to have memory projection, ability to move matter, to communicate a long distances with animals and all other species. That was taken away fearing that if they continued to so this, override or overcome if you would the natural creatures who had not that type of development. That's one of the big fears about melanin because it tends to unite under higher frequencies.

Melanin can adapt to all kinds of frequnecies and cause the body in which it is contained or the material in which it is contained to also be adaptive. It would mean the uniting of all the twelve DNA strands. That's what would make people with melanin gods once more. Towards this end the synthetics, those that were created by other planets and brought here and even the councils from tyrants and maldeck sought to keep this from happening. And they combined with what is called the serpent people, which is related in the book of genesis, related in the popuga, related in the el Koran, related in many of holy texts again. The serpent people, the dracons from neberu, were set upside so if would ever happened what had happended to their species again would happen and they did not want it to happen. There is two combinations now. One the dinoids and the other again the serpents if you would. These reptoids and dinoids are a group of people who are mortise looking like reptiles and dinosaurs that walk upright and this is what you have heard many times before.

The humanoids are a pattern of usually people or creatures with soul who wish to go to various sun systems to learn are the ones that are opposing. And this battle is also been going on for some time and the only reason why noth haven't annihilated each other that there are even higher species from places like lyra and other places again called the els or light benders. What it is an l shape and they bend light at ninety de-

grees and travel on mind control rather than on space ships. They said that this would never happen so there has always been this opposition that is now presently reaching its zenith or a culmination point. The planets in our solar system have various names. Not those names are very important but Ill give you the list of names as I understand them to be. Using what we can the names that we already understand. There are twelve planets in our system Mercury, Venus, Earth, Mars, Satania, Jupiter, Vulcan, Saturn, Uranus, Neptune, Pluto, and Clarion. These are all the twelve systems again. Each one carrying a different vibrational resonance and the different vibrations of light so that under the sun they create the twelve spectrums of light which causes a solar system to stay stable. Once that light is altered or either those planets began to send out less frequency then the ability to crash or to be sent off or shunted off grows.

And this is where you have the talk of asteroids and meteriors. Asteriods again are formed presently in what is called the earth's asteroid belt or our system's asteroid belt. That asteroid belt was formed only 52,000 years ago. It was the residue of maldeck and malona that formed a concentric circle in orbit of what was left and an asteroid belt when a sun changes the asteriods are then drawn off into the sun and disintegrated. But on their journey to the sun in many cases they would explode or they might collide with moons and other planets and cause a lot of serios damage.

This is why when this frequency changes with the sun, it is up to each planet to balance its electromagnetic field. Once that done then a ring is formed much like what is around Saturn and which earth is now forming also and they don't want to tell you about it. The frequency of that ring balances out the equator which means the inner sun of all planets can now shine through the openings which we now call poles. There are no poles there are simply openings. And that planet is now balanced for all life forms. It can balance again and wobble if necessary but it will not be sent out or shunted out of its orbital path. And it will reject meteors and

ateriods because its field is too strong. But without that world and collision like cosby talked about cant happen because there is no repulsion field there, because the planet is not balanced.

Our planet in order to be balanced is taken into what is called a photon belt. A belt of energy that will cause an artificial balancing at which time the asteroid belt can then be broken up and people on earth and people within the earth can be safely sent though because its been stated that the suffering that is going on here and all the advanced people that have had to come here to make this a reality. There should be a reward. So now to work through that is like a double or triple promotion. For some it's a double promotion, for others it's like a triple promotion because were been taken to what is called the Siruis section of our galaxy, where again the double really triple sun. The sun in sirius again will now be now that will be our new sun and pretty soon well find that we have three suns out there instead of one. Because we have actually would have changed positions.

Before that can be done people whose vibration is slow, that are holding back progression of the planet must be dealt with. They are given choices. First of all sucide if they would like because there is no such thing as death, just transition, annhilation, if you wish to try at wars, changing their own frequency by artificially setting up different kind of organisms or beginning to mutate themselves by raising consciousness. Any of those choices are left to the individual. All of those things are being presently practice on this planet.so if it sounds like what I said is crazy look around to the nueroticness that is going on around if you don't like the word crazy. They are making and creating and killing and having wars and rumors of wars and they are cross pyhluming and they are even raining through what they call the bat bath from alderbarron not so much the reticula. And the bat bath bath which we created on our own earth is now called greys.

It's a species of cancer if you would, it's a species of robots and people who can no longer can produce themselves. They only can do it through

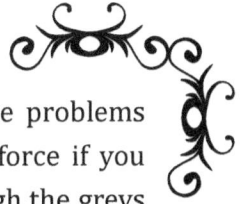

cloning, which go around balancing off planets just before problems come. They are like problem solvers.the are like a police force if you would. They are not independently strong they work through the greys and reptiods who of course anytime a person sees a reptiod or again a dinoid they freak out. So consequently these are like their planet preparers. These are the ones that come when a planet is going through a lot of change. What I have said to you is really way out. But what you are going to start reading in the papers and hearing on the radio and seeing is going to be even more way out. Because as I talked about in some of the other classes they have perfected here halography. They have prepared you for it by virtual reality. Halography was even practiced in the gulf war, the practiced in the seventh day war with Egypt in isreal is the ability to project through different kind of beam polarities in the sky on the gassiest cloud or a vapor cloud an image which seems real. Since many of the religious people are looking for a messiah, a return of a person to lead them in, they will produce that image.

People will think that they are seeing visions in the sky of the creator, of a messiah, of Allah, of Jesus, of Jesus (Spanish name for Jesus), whoever it is of Buddha. It will simply be a scientific production as they already have done. And they first practiced through the Israeles in the sixth day war in which you had a whole 107 tank commanders in the Egyptian army in a valley captured by three tanks and fifteen jeeps with sub machine guns. And of course they said these people were cowards, they were not cowards. And they had already sworn to oath and many of these were shiietes who were not afraid of anything, especially not death. But they put a hologram in which they thought that they saw a huge spaceship and they saw Allah as a vision.And while they were coming out genreflecting and huming they simply captured it. They can now produce realities that are not real.

They have already produced a false moon right here in Chicago. If you remember back last year one side of town saw a moon that was full and it had a color to it red. And the other people didn't see anything at all. They

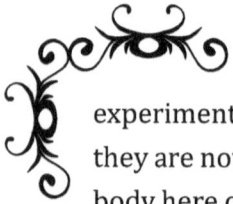

experiment with peoples minds all the time because the technicains that they are now serving are more alien in their concept and don't want anybody here on earth to evolve that could become to be rulers of the world or so again. It would come through a melinated person. Toward this end of they will do anything to stop that from happening. This is a time of great decision. It's a time when people must go with their own inner thoughts. There are people who this kind of lecture and thought they would have walked out a long time ago.

Some people still do. But it's not a matter of what Im saying. What I have tried to do is I have tied together you a package which will explain events that will be happening. This Monday NASA would supposedly if they are allowed to with golden again who is also a Jewish person which is the people that kept the covenant but not ruling the Jews. They hold control because they understand the inner gods of the inner world, and they honor them. And because of that they are given power. So much so that the people who used to be able to do it don't even know who they are and have stepped into a false religion. Consequently they have no psychic power that can converge little by little that thought has been given back. If they allow a true image to be resonated from Sedona on Mars, it will show the face of a black Negroid woman. It will also show a face again of a city which was built in a hexagon pattern and latter on in a pentagon pattern.

And it will show that within beneath there is a symbol that the marshians who are there live under the ground. There are marshains already here in the pentagon. There are marshains that serve in government. There are marshains a little bit of everywhere again. The only point is we have looked from people from space not to look black or Negroid. Therefore we don't look for Negroid aliens. The same mistake that I made. We find again that there are extra terrestrials and there are aliens. An alien could be an insectiod which is called scree, an alien can be a reptile or a dinoid. It can be any creature that usually becomes bipedal if given a chance to reach its highest. Anything that you can imagine. If you take a

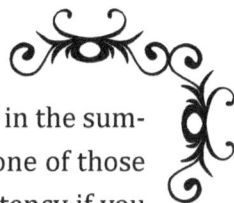

shovel and you dig in your backyard you will find in that soil in the summertime again 50 billion different kinds of life forms. Each one of those can be made if allowed to to grow to its true potential or potency if you would.

So, the whole point is again now we have more or less of a balancing act that is happening now and whatever form of light it wants to develop peacefully hopefully and wants to develop to its highest potency is now given that chance to do so. Our earth's electromagnetic field is being altered. Each day it is changing. I have already explained to you the weather that we are having is not real weather. Its weather that has been formed by the Russians and by certain factions of the Iluminati and the Natzis who went them to develop Nicholi Teslas what they call the resonating frequency. Resonance is now the new thing. It overrides magnetism and it overrides electricity. But our planet which is too electric stopping people from living long, causing people to be imbalanced, and causing a blackout of the mind is now changing to a magnetic field. They are going to tell you the exact opposite. They are going to tell you that the planet is getting a strong electrical field.

If it has a strong electrical field then the blackouts and brownouts, which you are going to see shouldn't be happening. And it means if it is electric there shouldn't be any power faliures as there are all the time and you are going to see more and more of it. It shows again that they are also lying. Our planet is becoming magnetic and on the magnetic frequency the only people that will be allowed to live on the surface are the ones with melanin or some kind of adapting artificial melanin that can adapt to different frequencies. That's why now, had child murders the Orange County murders as they try to make synthetic melanin. And they try to adapt again with whole new skins and whole new blood systems to live on the planet earth.

The planet earth is rejecting those who are not spiritual and who cannot form a magnetic blood and magnetic field. Those that have enough science would try to offset even what is being dictated through the suns

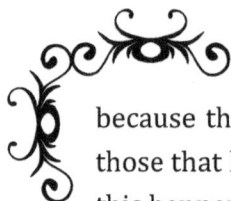

because they are not sons of the son, they are not soleman. There are those that live away from the sun and dont want to follow orders. All of this happens at a time when many of the things that are in our solar system are changing, that many of the things in the universe are changing, and that of course people's thoughts are changing. The idea that art bell can come on and keep people up all night long of all races and creeds mean its time for it.

At the same time you have a strong opposition who serves what they call the satanic forces. They might even be religious people because they are following a certain line of thought that makes people have to go outside of themselves to contact their creator. As we will talk about next week all you have to do is go within yourself and contact the creator, because if you have a soul that is part of the sun system which combines or calls a whole new central sun that becomes that like the creator. But toward the end there are those who don't have that progressive ability who want to stop that from happening. They will continue to send you radioactive devices. And they will tell you they want bigger and better TV pictures, bigger and better computers, and bigger better websites so they can monitor you and send through that website whatever it is they want to contaminate your own frequency. Your phone can be easily melted or tapped. It will. The lights can be taken out and changed. Animals are beginning to see better than some people because they are using their inner sight. It is now a time for inner sight. As you go along with this for a very long time, but I know just one of the many hundreds of things I said in the last hour or fourty five minutes probably you want to address or say something about. I will only say this. My contact was made back in 1960 as I put in record 18 years later. Having seen three saucers myself and seeing what they are capable of doing I was very impressed.

My only thing as I said on the tape was I was so juvenile and so unknowledgeable that when these people were black I rejected them because I couldn't understand a black man being a God. But if we now understand the dogans, the people from nubia, the people from Egypt and

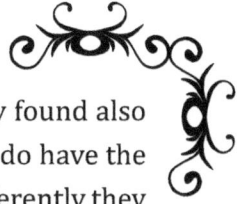

so did the same until they made the same mistake until they found also that not only people from mars, but people form siruis who do have the welfare of people here at state because some people look differently they have to wear camoflauge skins, they have to look a little bit differently. There is also a faction that does not like earth people and does not like anything that is Syrian or Niberian or anything else. They just simply want to rule the world and rule the galaxy. They contact those who they like. Saucers are real, ventlas are real. And one other thing that I didn't put in which I do want to. You will hear a lot of talk about chupracobras, about yeates, about abominable sonwmen, about Bigfoot. These were simply ancient people from maldeck who had souls in our solar system and because of this they had a penalty. They had to become what they call the guardians of the way who were made to reincarnate.

They were given Greta bodies of beasts with very intelligent insight and sometimes telepathic minds, a psychic mind. They were there to protect the inner ways, the gate ways to the inner earth where many of the people from other planets and many of the people who have escaped the deuage lived. They were put there to be gaurdians and to act in penance to make sure what they did would never happen again. They are very intelligent species. Somewhat telepathic, but they are bound into bodies for a certain time but reach dispensation until they undo what they did or help others to undo what they have done. They are called of course many of these creatures by various names. Some of the other creatures you will find are simply being made in laboratories within the earth itself by both aliens and again people without souls, or people who are already synthetics.

And I think you know who those people are again as the go into dolce and the vaious places I named last week in their laboratories to create new species, cross phylums, and to work with reptoids and dinoids toward what they call subjugation and once more the people of Shawn or the people of the earth. Anything you can imagine now can probably happen and is happening on this planet. But for a person with melanin

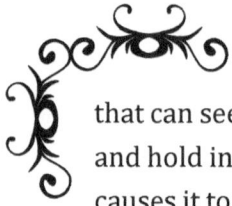

that can seek residence with thoughts or things. What you begin to think and hold in unison happens, good or bad. What you fear by thinking of it causes it to happen. Rejection on our very high frequency of a planet that has a very high magnetic field has a thought and it can keep away creatures or bring creatures to you. It can protect you or cause again things not to protect you. Thoughts are things. And just as we found now people can firewalk because their thoughts let them know that they are not physically and physical matter corresponds to mind. Mind does not let any harm come. It is unified thought, but everytime that you fear, everytime that you have your melanin contaminated with serums, everytime you do anything to lessen the vibration, you are not in harmony with the planet, the planet will not serve you. You are therefore unprotected.

Non protection is a matter of mind and a matter of thought. And each individual thought is capable of bring about reality. Virtual reality is what they tried to show you. We are already in virtual reality, because we are carrying everybody else's though but our own. And when we seek our own thoughts we are getting into religion, chemicals, or some kind of other rulership. This allows our privelage of doing so. Im not speaking as a black man very proud of being black. Im speaking of a galactic person, a soul who has the same karma you have that wants to see right done. Good is in blacks, good is in whites, good is in browns, good is in reds, because they have all now cross mixtured. Bad is in brown, black, white, red, and even the green people who were again found to be some form of caucasion who can change form green color to one of the inner worlds if you want to call it here, one of the tunnel systems, to a kind of pinkish color.

They are one of the only ones that can change from green to pink. This is their form of melanin. Everything here is confusion because truth has been layed barren. Truth here is not what has been taught. We have races here because we needed races. We had to find out again that there were different races in the cosmos. We have religion because we need religion. It was not enough to understand that you could go within and

be what you wanted to be. We have governments because we refuse to govern ourselves. And we need policeman because we tried to cheat and we needed someone to protect us. Once you lived on a true sun vibration and are allowed to exist under a sun, you will find all of that is usesless because you remember everything that you do. And at the time of transition, it is all recorded and you judge yourself, then what you have to do again to get it straight. That is what is meant by reincarnation under a sun. There is nothing new under the sun and being earth bound. Nobody would be allowed to be earth bound after this dispensation.

You either will go someplace else and try it again or you will be given the triple promotion of going into the Sirian system and what is called the galactic confederation away from the things that are enemies, away from the things that hold you back because you have earned it the hard way because you become incarnate on the planet earth. I could go on and on with this. But I wont. Ill simply say again I know it's a hard pill to swallow or it might be a pill that you like to taste. Either way I can judge it by your questions and comments. And I thank you very much!

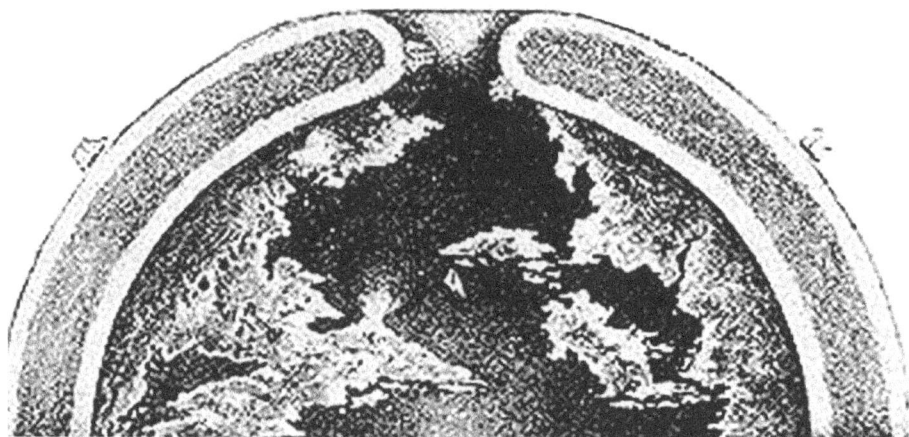

The World Within
Part 5-1

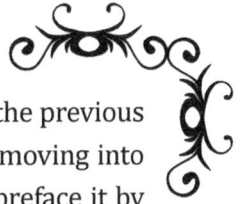

*I*f you have attended or bought the previous tapes for the previous four sessions, then you will understand how we are moving into part five as we now go the world within you. And I preface it by simply saying understand the explainable you explain the understandable. You look at what you can comprehend to understand what is not supposed to be comprehendable and we find again as time moves on everything becomes rivitingly clear. The site of one of the greatest earth pyramids which originally named el cahira, el cahira. It's from the Arabic word called el cahir which means mars. It was so again named in the tenth century by the same pope and those that visited with the pope that named the continenet of kemet Africa. A misonomer of one and a true name of the other.

There is no such thing as the continent of Africa. It is only Kemet and have many other names. In fact the old continent at one time was called ethopia and the sea there which we now call the Mediterranean Sea was called the Ethoptic Sea. Another time was called Kemet or Kemit. So as we are finding out that we have been lied to in history about most of the thigs that we have been taught and if not complete lies and enough mistruths and enough misgivings to make most of what have learned have to be subject to scrutiny. To say that it was called Mars this whole pyramid and the whole plateau and defined now through dissertations and programs that are coming on the radio and books that are being published that this same kind of structure and the classical sphinx is now also fined in an area in Sedona on Mars.

It begans to change the concept about what a lot of people have thought before and what a lot of people are thinking. You will Africa is going to be in the news for the rest of the year and into new century. The true name will soon be given and the areas there of concern there will be of course Lake Killamanjaro of course Lake Victoria, the Giza plateau, and the Nile which was reversed. And they want to understand who and what made the Nile flow backwards and what kind of power can do that. We are going to find soon that the Sphinx on mars and the Sphinx here in the United States has Negroid features.

They were blown off by Napoleons eighth granadears of course here and there on mars they were eroded through an accident that happened with Maldeck and Malona which we talked about exstensively last week. To understand this entire presentation today you need to go back to the series you may have missed and we urge you to do that as soon as possible. I have here of course some pictures that were taken form a number of magazines and a number of books. And one of the pictures that I want to show here of course is the pharoah tutankahman which is in this book called Pharoahs, another one of the pictures comes from another book Africas Gift to America J.A. Rogers, one of the mini series.

And this particular picture shows again the artist's rendition in Napoleons 1798 expedition shows of course the black looking sphinx before they desecrated it. On the other side again you see the sphinx Negroid looking and then the restorations and so as they actually go up to supposedly restore what is defaced. They understand quite well that the pyramid and sphinx were not built at the same time. We have mistold of course it is all apart of the same structure. It was not. The pyramids could have been built anywhere from 15000 B.C. to 11000 B.C. That would be the pyramind. The sphinx was built anywhere from 10800 B.C. to 8700 B.C. Neither of those represents the 2680B.C. that the finder's petree misguided and told us it was probably built there. I have here just a couple of these stone sections to see the tonnage that was used in the sphinx.

There is some two million five hundred blocks of stone in the pyramid alone. Of that there are six granite giants that weigh close to three hundred tons each. And there are close to a million and half that weigh close to 75 to 150 tons. No men moving, gang planks and ropes and mules and whatever else again and pulling by that they have ever built that. You have heard my tape on that. If you haven't just go get any of the other tapes I have on the great pyramid. Obviously now the technology used was tremendous. And of course the same technology that they using on

mars sent a red bell alert all over the planet for people of course who don't want people who make sphinx that look like negroids to be capable of such that ought to be idolated.

So still somebody went through all that trouble to make it look like them. Either way it's a no no. It's a yes yes for me because it's what I believe in for a long time. That's why I never got tenure. That's why I walked away or got fired from just as demanding many a job or school position. And since I said I was not going to lie to any young mind that I was trying to reach, that's why I went on my own. So it's a heavenly day for me, but I also know what precludes this and what also follows. And for that Im not too happy about. We will be getting into all of that now if you will. On the sheet of course as we are going to take a very long look at the whole idea of the shinx and the whole idea of the pyramid itself. The story stated that on top of the Great pyramid, which again is a four sided an equilateral triangle there was a capstone.

And the capstone was made of either gold or some precious metal that resembled gold and it had within it the eye of Horus, which represented of course the all seeing eye. It meant that there was a golden cap to all of that structure and it was a huge crystal within that. And that was a power unit. That was the top power unit which would balance the other power unit that was hidden under the ground. So when they took that away the pyramid no longer functions. And this is why it was reffered to as a tomb. No one was ever buried there purposely. It was never an entombment for Kufi, micronanas or anyone else or chiaps if you mispronounced it as the Greeks did.

It was simply again a structure that was a dynamic generator and a telecope an observatory all in one and even a landing coordinant or like you might say a control tower. Once they took away that part it no longer functioned as it could and so therefore we have had vestiges of a mighty structure that some very intelligent life forms had obviously built. When it is restored and when it beguns to work again it will cancel out all energies on the planet earth as far as using electricity. Because it will gener-

ate directly from the sun which is now becoming magnetic which means electricity would not work until the year 2000 into the millennium. Electricity is the thing that has held most people back here. This is called radiation and poison and it must go. Magnetism will replace it. In a sense that saying spirituality will replace pragmatism.

And this is why they are having a battle now that is going on. People that are very pargamatic, materialistic, who are very spiritual and want the magnetic frequencies to do things with the mind, what they used to do but the power is taken away because the power reperesents the skull of man. Now when I say the skull of man you must understand something else. We will be getting into that next week. The skull of man does not mean the skull of human. It does not mean the skull of woman, it does not mean the skull again of mankind. It means the skull of man, just that. Man being a group of people that were given to planet earth as a habitat to see if they could work out their problems and procreate again into a new concsciousness. This whole story of course was taken away as it was talked about in many cases through the bible. And when the new religion of Christianity was given to people and that's exactly what it was a new relgion of christainity. And I hope Im not stepping on some feelings but youre going to have lots of feelings stepped on in the next two years. Ah what Im simply doing is to tell you the truth as I understand it. I wouldn't lie to you knowingly.

As I have always said if you find a lie come back and tell me cuz I run my mouth too much now on many stations so on and like this. And I want to change that and do something about it. The capstone of the great pyramid represents the skull fixture of mankind and the skull itself of man. As we know when we are born and we sill get into this more next week the skull sutures and the hole that was at the top now closes. And that's when the little soul now gets illumination. They now have the five senses. They have lost three other senses at that point. They become captured if you would. And the gland that sits most near the top of the skull is the pineal gland.

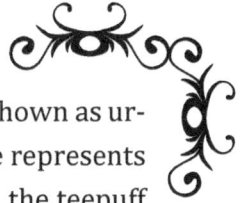

The pineal gland is your master gland which was always shown as ur-asis when you see the great pharaohs again. Urasis of course represents the little serpent or snake that sticks out on the forehead on the teepuff on most of the pharaohs again we see. There are usually two one being like a hawk figure and a cobra and the other small. Represents again wave. Snake serpents have waves and coils. It represents energy coming and going. The ablity to be psychic, grounded, and pragamatic at the same time. The duality of man. The duality of man is not found in human. Human is in grafted man, the beast man, the animal man. This one represents an awakened conciousness and the use of power and therefore they were looked at as phaorohs or rooters. The fraos is of course is what their names were but they were called pharaohs mistranslated by the Greeks. There are many words that are not correct, but we have been mistaught.

And being mistaught of course you can not blame ignorance because it is those who knew the truth that didn't tell who would be the blame. We look even more so into this whole idea of the capstone and the sphinx. And we find that the pyramid within our own bodies is very much alive and working. But the two units that make it work best is the pineal gland which is a big crystal. It takes in light during the day time and reflects it back at night especially between the hours of ten thirty and two thirty on the natural cycle not daylight savings and other cycles again. The natural cycle. And again as we have told you many times why we like the noni juice becasue it will continue to titilate that pineal gland and have it began to work through the pituitary gland which works through all the other organs and glands which keeps us seated in a body. Hoping in this car or truck that we call our body and make it function correctly so you can hit all gears. Without that you are either going in reverse, you are going in half gear, half speed, you can't accelerate too well.

Within the pyramid itself of course they talked about the grand gallery. And the grand gallery was supposedly a large entrance way in the pyramid that went up the side. And if you can possibly see from there and

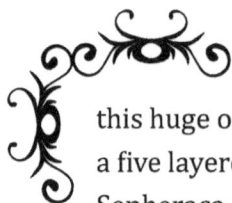

this huge opeining there up to what is called the kings chamber which is a five layered column or four columns of course in five layers over above Sepheraca which of course which was beneath it and the pharaoh was said to have been buried. Well they stated that they never used this for a tomb. Nobody was buried there period.

If they were there it's because they fell and died, but not because they were buried there. What this represents is a huge generator or slycatron if you will. And one of the byproducts of that was to clean what is called the electromagnetic field to make you well and whole. It got rid of any conditons in your body as a by product. This was not its main function. It was just one of the things that you did when you had some time to do while you were working at the great pyramid bringing in spaceships and coordinating things in the underworld and all like this. Just like you might say a spa if you would. No more or no less. Crystals used to line the grand gallery. And when all of these crystals were in place and the sound resonance was hit it would send out light and sound through the two shafts at different times or the grade or depending on who they were trying to contact and how far they had to send the signal.

And of course for people to work in here they had to be very syncrinated, their blood stream had to be well, they had to have high vibrations because just the tone itself would drive some people out of their mind if theyre brains were more practical and if you want to call it pragmatic and if occipital lobe was not developed enough. So it automatically tells you what kind of people had to work in this and the kind of conditions that they had to work under again. The seperca was one where it was not made for a body at all. It was made for a unit known as the arc of the covenant. There are eight such units planets still on the planet earth. Two of them now are trying to be possessed bythe Jewish people who have not been able to successfully do anything with it.

The one it still remains is in Ethopia.Thats also a pundit, because Ethopia used to be the name of the entire continent. You must understand that it was rightfully thus the people were still there had it and no

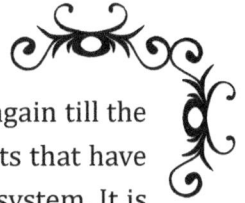

one else there can make it work anyway. And it can't work again till the capstone is in place and certain resonances on all the planets that have negroid looking people now began to function back in this system. It is not that Negroid people are so great. Please don't misunderstand me. It's because again they were generally the surface people and the people that could go from the underworld to the surface because of melanin. And that why melanin and melanin research is so prime. And I again caution you about giving up your melanin through these shots and spinal taps. Its one of the worst things that you could do at this time. I always have to throw that in.

If you have it you have been blessed. Use your blessing well. It's been a long fight to get you to understand what that blessing is worth. When we are also looking again at the idea of whats goimg on you must understand that the story had been told and retold many cases. If the and Im not going to get into a long thing on this, I have a whole tape called the two stories of Christainity. But the so called Christian fathers in 325 A.D. met and created the whole relgion that we have come to know christainity. What they displaced or replaced was the ancient religion again of the oneness of man and all the creations, that fact that we are in classrooms, the fact that we are sometimes fought over, and the fact that this planet was set aside where all the particular planet in life could see if they could live in harmony. Obviously that is failed. But one of the things that was done was to show that these great souls thought that they understood what they could do and knew their power to see what could be done if they have power taken away and power was given to those who had no power to see again if people could actually live in haromony and they were equal. And of course the equality of all that was still unequal because melanin was not granted to everybody, which limited where they could travel on the planet without getting sick, without getting imbalanced, without getting diseased, in and out of balance again.

Melanin automatically lets you travel anywhere on the surface of earth and even into the interior of earth in perfect balance because when it is

functioning corectly it causes a higher vibration to be secreted through the pituitary gland for all of the organs and glands and hormones in the body and you automatically adjust. Well find soon that as we travel wherever in the galaxy or the cosmos is not a matter of how you get someplace. That's easy. It's a matter of adjusting when you get there to bring that reality in sequence. Other than that you are morted. This is the key vibrations and resonance, vibrations and resonance. We have been taught only vibrations. The key behind vibrtation is resonance. Resonate frequency if you will.

The crucification as was being given by the passion plays and Easter which was honored of course a couple of weeks ago was that Jesus the Christ or the Christ Christos, the annointed one was crucified. And of course many things were said about the crucification. But at the crucification it was between two thieves who asked one day again and they said supposedly one day or this you will ascend with me to heaven. Even though they had been thieves and robbers and all like this, the crucification was a hardest way to explain. And of course he was crucified in the land of gogartha, near the mountain of gogartha. And you know the rest of that story. I won't bore you with that story again. But you must understand the metaphysical resononace of that metaphor.

All things that we are taught is on seven levels. Everything that we learn is on seven levels. We are only going to hit about the first three. So understand that there are even more meanings behind this. Seven levels of everything here on this planet. Seven stages of consciousness. Seven understandings. Take one if you want, but don't believe that that is the ultimate. Because its too many mansions in the fathers house and too many things that we need to learn. To understand the crucification you must understand another principle. And that principle is symbolized in the Kaducias. And the Kuducisas is simply well again the idea that again man is seated in the chamber of life and that the true robber serpents found on each side of the crucification simply represents the umipangala numigastic nerves and all that goes with it. Simply again those that

send the energy upward refraining from sex, refrain form fighting and refain from anamalistic activity which produces a fluid that goes into the medulla stem and the other nerve center if you will on the right hand side simply sending it back down again so man cannot ascend. The sixteenth vertebra represents where the fluid changes and represents the power man has laiden within him again. To find again the pyramid and the sphinx on the same plateau at giza simply shows that the people understood exactly what they were doing, exactly what they were building , and understood the metaphysical as well as the very practical . Something that everyone alive on earth now is supposed to do to understand the pragmatism and materialistic concept, but to have enough power and spirituality to still bring out the other portions of ones nature.close your eyes as a group and I want you to keep them closed until I ask you to open them again. By doing this we all will be in sync and coordinated . Then Im going to ask you a question when you open your eyes. Please just answer the question if you will. Ill ask each of you a question

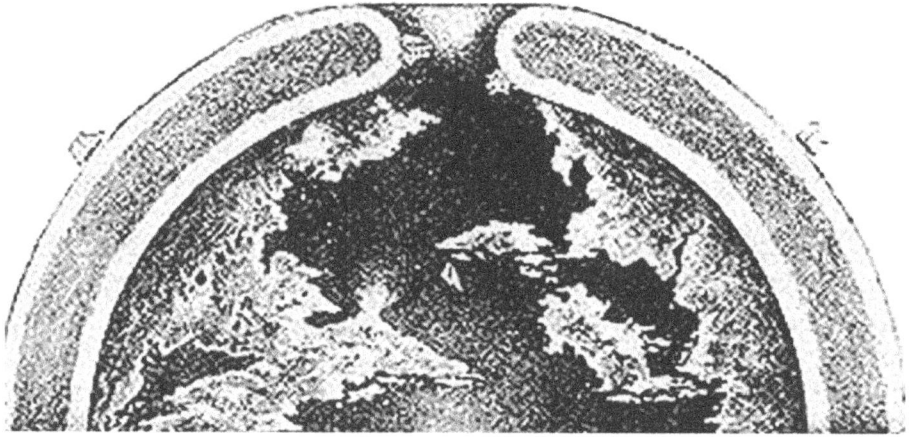

The World Within
Part 6-1

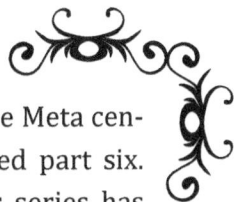

*T*odays lecture for Saturday April the 25th at the Meta center again is the world within series continued part six. And its now deeper worlds within you. Our series has gone very deeply to all worlds within our planet. Are we in the human body itself? And today is no exception. We will be covering things about the chakras, womb man, the truth about your newborns, the phrase the worm turns, the bow unk inceptor, and hopefully a little about the human aura. This is continuing series and the metacenter mailing address is 1448 East 52nd St, Chicago, IL 60615. The phone number is 773 643 5053. We hope again that you will contact us at the center and we hope you enjoy the presentation again. I want to start I guess with the idea about wombman, of course we all know woman is not pronounced wombman. And so comes the connotation why and why the saying wombman. Well that goes on of course metaphysical research. And the metaphysical research is one that says that the universal hemaphradite, the original androgen the original wombman is the real race of man. That original man is wombman. Now I say that simply because wombman has two secret glands that are scientist, pysiologists, and teleopathic doctors do not talk and tell her about.

We have talked about of course for some time now over use of estrogen and hystorectomies and ovarian removals and tubligations that woman has thrown her hormonal system off. And just as they didn't teach woman that the ovaries not only secreted estrogen, but a form of progesterone and to replace it with just estrogen is to make it one sided to create a problem. Well one of the things that they have not told and probably soon will probably doing the wombman lecture again that probably about when I have the ladies over for six hours and then I know if I do that all the men will show up. And we'll get into some of the deeper things that usually can't be talked about or wont be talked about. But Ill simply say for today without going into huge detail that the two secret glands that woman have. One is call the epufiron and the other is paroufiron. The epufiron and the paroufiron. The epufiron is also known as the

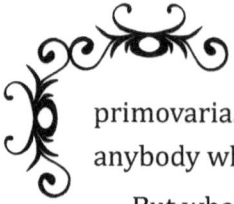

primovaria. You will hear that more or less in general physiology talk or anybody who is into or be in gynecology or so on like this, the epufiron.

But what they don't tell you is the epufiron manufactures sperm cells and that the paroufiron can manufacture seminal fluid and sometimes sperm cells itself. That within the female is the capability of manufacturing sperm as well as eggs. Here is the proof of that, simple this or if there is anthing that can become proof. Both are encased within what is called the mesoso sphinx. The mesoso sphinx. This is one of the secrets of the great sphinx again. They say it usally fast so its messosfix. Buts its mesoso sphinx. And this is again that raw ligament which is folded around the ovaries. Of course the female has two ovaries. It forms which is known as the versa evatacus. The versa ovatacus or the ovarian sac. Now you have therefore male testicular tissue producing spermatozoa in juxta position to the female ovary right in the female body. This goes back to the original what is called hermaphrodite.

The universal androgen or androgenous being having male and female piston stigma on the same cluster or stem. This is how the universal man was here. Man of course was taken from woman. Not woman from man. This is a biblical change over for a patriarchial society that wanted to rule and wanted to take over. And all you have to do is ask yourself if woman stop having babies where would man be. Man cannot reproduce himself other than through cuttings. Much is he is doing now through what is cloning. You come through the birth canal and be born of a spiritual nature. Having a spiritual vestige you have to then go to a wombed man the man with the womb. The man without womb is a degenerate species and this is one of the reasons that they do a lot of circucison and all like that.

I don't want to further with that part but just letting you know that that is a major reason for a lot of female problems. And a lot of reason for the mental problems between males and females, especially when that balance is not taught and people get upset. Those are again starting off with a bang. The two secret glands that women has, Man has two secret

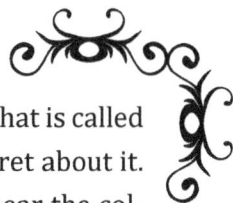

glands too only one of which I will share tonight and that is what is called his pineal gland. Now everbody says well that's nothing secret about it. You check back in your books at the medical societies and near the colleges and universities and youll find that going back in the early eighties in some cases in the middle eighties, they had very little to say about the pineal gland. In fact they said it's an atrophied gland, ganglar residue of very little use and has no function. Well that's like saying your eyes and your ears have no function. If you take away those two senses and see how you get about it now. So I guess what I am simply saying is that we have been told a lot of tales.

The idea is that in the great sphinx and especially the pyramid was a secret of male and female.And the secret of course was man's secret gland which was his pineal gland. Because if you notice again, Ill go the blackboard later . I want to make it in continuity here. When you remember from last week, when you go up the grand gallery in the entrance way to the sphinx, there is one level by which you supposedly go to the queen's chamber. And then above it with the peek roof, five planes I think in masonry they say the five levels, the king's chamber with the open sepercure. Well the sepercure was never supposed to be containing anybody's body. It was to contain a unit, an electrocalmaganetic thing which they called the arc of the covenant. Similair to that is what you find in a persons skull. And man not human and not mankind but man has a reverse hole in the roof of the mouth, which leads up to the nasal passage ways. And there is a big opening this is why you can eat something and you see it come through the nose if it comes the wrong way.

Or if you have eye ear connection because all these opnings come right in the back and they lead up. You can swallow it goes to the ears, it goes to the eyes. All of these are open pathways. There are eight of them and of course the skull itself is nothing but an open residency chamber which is what the pyramid is when it functions correctly, a residency chamber. All of the sinuses that we have within the skull, these openings are made to feel vibrations and feel and sense air. Even in heat and cold the ma-

gantism and electricity in the air is sensed by these openings. When they stop up we get asthma we get sinusitis. All these kinds of things.

And everything that we are told to eat stops us up. Everything we are told to drink stops up those passage ways. With the male that opening is supposed to be kept open for except three days out of the month. And during that time, a secrertion, like a woman has a menses that comes down that channel that is supposed to drop into the throat and stimulate the body to go into a higher frequency usually causes a male to want to eat during that time, its very sensitive during that time.And it is a resonancy with the same kind of thing that happened within the pyramid.

They took away the crystals in the pyramid. They took away the vibrations that used to rush down from the top and down to the bottom through the pyramid beneath the pyramid. In this case it took away the opening in the top of our heads which also it is where they have what is called the crown shakra which we will be talking about. And the little pathway through the pons veroli down to what they call the trescarshia, the little saddle bone there in which the pituitary gland lies there and it hangs on a little limb like from the pineal gland. It's almost like a little resonancy, alittle clock ticking back and fourth.When this thing begans to vibrate you began to get psychic and you began to send forth energy through what is called the shsusharata or the top crown shakara and you also began to engergize the emf field like I demostrated last week.

That's how you can begin to energize that. But also there makes a matter of your blood. Your blood changes vibration when that happens becsause the blood is manufactured of course through the bone marrow and the hemoglobin capabilities and the oxygen capability. But all of this is controlled through what, the pituitary gland. But where does pituatry so called master gland take its marching orders from, the pineal gland. So this whole thing was kind of shown in a pyramid, because whe they took away the capstone of the pyramid, and when they then took away the crystal of the capstone the pyramid no longer functions. Its dead thing.That's what made them understand when they talked about the

dead osirus that this was now a place for the dead. It didn't mean that it was a burial place. Itr meant that the life force that it used to give forth is now gone.

And it's dead. Most of us are dead. The third eye went out the little light goes out. And you notice again if you are on a fast and you are drinking a lot of juices, you breathe in deeply, the eyes began to shine. There is a glow that comes to the skin. You can't miss it. Anybody that goes on a fast you can tell that. Or they clean up their diet. And then when you eat the meats and the pastas the little light goes out and gets very dull. You look at an animal. A cat especially that is very finnicke about what they eat. Their eyes shine and the pupils will open and dialate almost so they look as like a reptile. Because they can work both sides of the fence because they are very capable.

Even in dogs again when you give them a lot of food, little puppies they shine. They will shine in the dark. That shows that they have a soul. That shows that they have a pineal gland, they have soulforce, they have what is called superior continuity. They have the understanding of being able to go to a higher vibration. Once we get centered into the animal plane that little light goes out. Its dull. You notice drug addicts and peope who are very obeast, their eyes are dull.

Because all of the glands have been clogged up. All of the resonancy holes in the skull, their full of asthma, full of pneumonia, all the choloracy, everything is stopped up. And that means the whole vibrational figure eight of the blood is now a lower vibration. So I say all that simply to say when man understands who he is, he honors that hole through his mouth and he honors what he eats, what he doesn't eat, he honors what he thinks and doesn't think.

And mainly that little hole as I say is left open then the body tries its best to release what is called the golden elecxic. Last week we talked about how we brought it up the spine. This is what happens again. There are two ways of doing it. Now I am not going to get into the other way. But that is the way it is supposed to be done. Once you do that the person

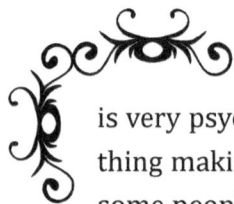

is very psychic, the person is very open and in tune and as soon as anything making mucous gets in there the body reacts to it. I have a habit, some people have got on my case. Well I spit a lot. Why in the world do you do that. When I learned that I almost went through a death crisis that when all those things get stopped up I can feel my psychic power going whenever I drink some milk or im going to eat some ice cream, ill get some bread or ill get something that's not supposed to be in there and gets in that little hole. I now can feel it. The first thing I want to do is discharge it.

I don't want to take any of that. Most people, most men its all clogged up anyway now. And they get sinus problems when they go to the steam room or they are swimming underwater. And that pooping sound that pressure gets so great,and all this muscous starts flowing out because its nothing else to release it. You go up in the air in an plane and get to about oh 28000 feet or more all that pressure from the pressurization forces all that mucous out. For some it's just like hitting a stone wall. You dont have to worry about anything being forced out. It just rebound off it because their cemented tight. But for a person that can move mucous they start getting an ear ache, start getting the nose, the sinus problem.Because its trying to move that mucous out. That lets you understand the different vibrational rates of our planet.

The higher vibrations or as you get away from the central gravity pull toward the sun and therefore to go up that way your skull has to be open. Other than that that pressure shows that your not based now for heavenly existence your still down on earth you cant live up there physical body because the body is too clogged up. Its not resonancy chamber it cant adjust to frequencies its made now to walk the surface of the earth and that's about it. So, this is why you can't keep the body with you. The secret in man is that when he opens up that skull not only can he become psychic but he can began to sense himself and what to do for his body. Cause as I showed last week if you're in tune to any part of your body if you get quiet with yourself and listen to it. It would tell you what it

needs, it will tell you what to do. But if the delivery system is clogged up you still won't be able to do anything with it. It would just be there. So, again man can become god. Human will search for mankind. But it takes man and humans to tell humans and mankind who their godhead is.

They will search the planets for it. Its within themselves. If its not within themselves they are always still lacking that's why there war like, that's why they are very discovering. This is why they are trying to gain what they never had. Not at least on this planet, because this planet is like a test site. Its an experimental laboratory and everything comes here to learn truth. What they feel is a physical existence or a phscial plane. So that's the secret of mans secret gland. Woman secret gland. And that leads again to another conept that I would like to kind of go with. We are also told that when a woman is pregnant and delivers that the first born is after the union of sperm and egg is a zygote on the uterine wall which attaches and goes through supposedly nine months. And then after that during that nine motnths gestation period there is a fetus that is growing.

The fetus during the first three months looks like a tadpole and then it goes to something else again, and then born a baby. And of course the baby it's almost something that can't do anything almost till up about the sixth seventh or eight month. About the third to the fifth month the holes at the skull closes and then all the senses get more bright. And they so everything is well. Well that's a very interesting crinology and very interesting thing to know and not know. First of all all original zygotes are females. You will hear of allopathy. I would say mankind say that is not the truth. Secondly that the original zygote changes because of not only the production of progesterone and also how the pineal gland is working through the pitituary gland and the females thought.

Usually you can tell that thoughts were things because the female can mark the child during the first three months of pregnancy and then forming birth marks on the fetus. The fetus is chassy, I like to say chassy but you can call it the body what ever you would. Whatever the female

longs for its afraid of it, so its usually a pattern. The cells take on that pattern where she is actually marking with mental comciousness physical matter, which shows mind always controls the physical. That's why we had the mind seated in the body so we can take control of it. But we are not told this and we think the brain runs the body. If the brain runs the body, what runs the brain?

So the point is it is the soul or mind that is seated in the brain. And these are only little cars and buildings that we live in. Once you understand that then you honor the mind in the mindstream and this is where they say thoughts are things. You are taught on this planet as you think so shall you be. With that whole thing the idea is that the thought form that is to becme the child is around you longer before its born and may never get born. It depends upon the circumastances. But that thought form that soul consciousness, that mindforce that wants to get through to you whenever you come into physical existence is still part of you whether it becomes a fetus or whether its carried around without being fetal. That force that is around us is a form of energy that is caught up in our energy field that manifests usually at night in our dreams. And if sometimes the person begans to even dream in color, usually when that happens you began to dream of a mate coming and all like this. But we will be getting more into that next week. But the second thing that usually happens there is that when that soul is drawn in and actually becomes part of a zygote formation itself, it carries with it a complete thought.

It is a live creature in the elemental kingdom of earth and it is the elements that brought it about. Sperm and egg are nothing. Sperm and egg are catalyzer for elements and subatomic particals and all the energy that they convey. After they stimulate into grow then they require more of the elements. And the elements create more and more minerals and the vitamins because now it has to build what is called a coporial body. It's got to build a physical body from something that is done physical and for something. But that will best match the vibrations of the donors and the soul that needs to come in. The soul was already communicating

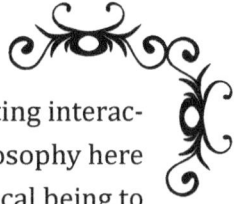

because on this existence here we have set up lots of interesting interactions. And we will get more into that next week but the philosophy here is that those interatcions sometimes will manifest as a physical being to further interact with that person that is now physical. Whether it be the mother or the father or both.

And that that zygote when being formed is nothing but a group of material cells growing until the time a soul makes entry. Another thing that metaphyscias teaches that our present science does not teach is that soul may come and go three or four times before that fetus is actually born. And that's why the woman's attitude will change three or four times a she carries until gestation. Souls they fight so hard not to get born but they will wait past the ninth month. Some souls are so anxious and they don't want a perfected body, they want a perfected brain and they will be born prematurely. And will make things happen or the two souls combine the female carrier and that's all she is and she is a catalyst and the soul trying to get in will sometimes work together to get that is a premature thing to happen.

Based on how much time that soul thinks or needs it has or the female thinks she needs and has. The fetus has always communicated and it communicates more before it is born more than the first two or three months after it is born. During the night especially when that pineal gland is working, the soul or the fetus of that energy will make contact with the woman. She will dream vivid dreams. They will have all kind of interchanges. This soul that is coming in and her, they will work out and argue about things. This is where these cravings come from when the woman knows maybe she needs a stronger pineal or she needs more of this to get the kind of soul she wants in. So these cravings will come in and if you notice in most cases because cow's milk has been our best form of calcium, the woman will usually crave things that will use up calcium, or the teeth will began to decay, or bones will get brittle.

Because the calcium that that soul needs has to combine woth the magnesium molecule to get a spiritual soul. Magnesuim alone can't car-

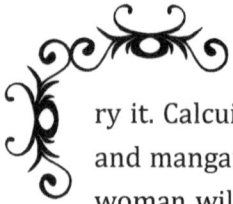

ry it. Calcuim alone can't carry it. So calcium, magnesium, phosphorus, and manganese are necessary to set up that kind of a food sac. And the woman will get cravings for these things but because of ignorance will not know what she she needs just get a craving. But she answers it by going out and getting a candy bar or going out and getting something so way out because that is mistaught. We are not told what fruits vegtables legumes and seeds carry the kinds of things that would be needed. But the soul that is here communicating its living in the same body and to share that temple and body they need extra of somethings.

And if you notice again if you don't feed that child or you don't feed that fetus again by the time you are born or so you are the healthiest you have ever been. Because before that time it would take calcium from your teeth take phosphorus from your hair. It will take anything you have got until you eat right to get it corrected. And it will just fall out because the baby is going to take it. But when you honor that ther is enough plurality, there is enough of everything for other things to be carried over and everybody can share. And of course the baby is always talking. It talks until the time it is born and then it can't talk. It talks psychically and mentally during those first three trimesters. And then when it is born it looses the ability to talk and its waiting for now vocal cords to grow and mature and to learn what it is supposed to say in the phycial plane. But the mother when she kind of becomes kind of rest broken and tuning onto the child at a distance in the next room, it knows exactly whats going on especially if they are intune. And of course if she is breast feed during that time, then communication is carried on in the form of RNA replication too because now the hormones are shared which makes it very much intune and they know exactly what is going on before.

So my point is that um the truth about a newborn and when does it think starts long before it even becomes a zygote, thinks while it is a zygote, thinks while it is a fetus, and thinks less before it is baby a least nine or ten months old. Becaue here is what happens.The soul is living as much on the other side of life, obviously their there right now as it is on

the so called understoosd physical side of life. Until the cranial suture do just that. The hole at the top of the head, the hole at the pole closes. It sutures and before that time it's a soft spot in the babys head. If you press it too hard or anything comes over it, you can do great damage to the child. Some of these forceps that they force these deliveries with, terrible because they press the cranial and sometimes force that hole closed.

This is a terrible thing. If you are sicilain, or if you were part of the uroba and so you didn't step over a baby. You didn't spend too much time with your root chakras over a babys crown chakra. We will be talking about that. Because you were acting in what they call harming a soul. Because they understood that as long as that hole was open the baby was receiving higher vibrations. That soul was still in communication with the other side if you will. But once that hole was closed the chamber was sealed, like they did the Great pyramid. Then it meant that the only way to get out of the body now had to be through astroflight. It has to be another path, becasuse the inner dimension of Jacobs ladder was now closed. It could climb in and out throught the spirit, psychic realm you will see what is called owning the physical realm. So when that closes what happens?

Now the baby can see well, it begans to talk, it can hear physical things but it looses the sixth and seven senses. The ability to see and hear vibrations and see sound and hear color and all these kinds of things. It becomes then an encased soul that is now earth born. Born of earth and that is what we want to see, earth born. Interesting enough they even have a terrible practice of putting silver nitrate in the birth canal when that child is coming down there. Because supposedly the silver like were teaching now kills off germs and things. But not silver nitrate, high vibrational liquid silver. The nitrate it ruins the eyes, it ruins the opothalamus nerve and the child is born with poor eyesight. So I am simply saying that obviously there are forces that understand this, because they have instituted a whole teller mentoring process of what we should be and what we should do.

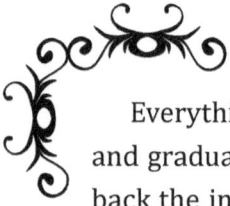

Everything that will retard advancing high entry vibrational points and gradually high vibrational entries. So in other words it tries to cut back the intelligence a soul can bring in with him and the kind of soul that we want to come in for that or if the soul insists in coming in it suffers. The answer to all of those again, thinking always goes on, communicating goes on, but at different levels than we have been taught. Its not just by speech, its not just by hearing. It's by feeling and resonance. So the truth about your new borns again, the only thing we will say about that one is the kind of souls that are coming in now are warriors. They are coming at this time. They don't know why they are coming, they are here for a purpose. They are aslo here to bring back to destiny the purpose that brought them back in the first place. Most of them are ol souls. Old souls back again to get it straight.

Especially any of them even thinking about being born in the last ten years. They are the oldest ones. There is a phrase that is used a lot saying the worm turns. I have that as interpreted you got a worm like individual and you back them into a corner and they then have to stand up, they turn. Its just like you backing any dog or cat or animal into a corner. A rat that lives will fight a lion if backed into the corner.Now a few of them will just turn over and have a heart attack. But most of them when you put in a corner, be prepared because they now know there is no way out and its just you and them and they want to inflict some damage or by miracle they will get away.

Well that's not what it means at all. It sounds good but it has nothing to do with the phrase. The worm turns is based on a very deep metaphysical teaching that was taught by the wizards and arts of old and by those who were students of metaphysical phiolosophy. And that is again that the pineal gland has a little ligament if you would that attaches to the pituitary. And the pituatry stands again in something that looks like a saddle. I will put this on the board. This is more or less for the listening audience. We will go over this on the visual.

But it looks like a saddle if you go over the old English saddle those side saddles as they called them. They had everything to brace the per-

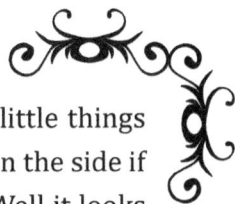

son. They had a front stirrup and a back brace and it was little things that went into the thing. And sometimes it was easier to sit on the side if you were a female because it was just like a little carriage. Well it looks the same thing. This bone has four legs to it if you will, it has a resting area and it kind of fits sideways again in the skull. This is where the pituitary is. But the piruatary hangs by ganglia cross wise in that saddle and it looks like a little worm. That's exactly what the pituitary gland looks like. Pineal gland looks like a pincone. That's why it's the pineal gland, not pinal. You will pay a penance for it for getting resonancy. The pine thing and of course its little ganaglias there. And if anytime the worm that little pituitary gland is trying to turn, its trying to turn again in that saddle. But because it grows bigger and the brain once that hole closes it also tightens up and that bone gets closer. There is no room to turn in. But it's constantly pulsing. The hottest spot on your body is always going to be the top of your head.

And it breathes up there just like your heart. Everytime your gets two palpitations it one breathe that comes here. Its called the breath of brown. That little suturing up there is always trying to cause a pressure on the pineal pituitary complex, the king and queen's chamber trying to get them to resonate and it's always trying to escape because it doesn't want to be locked down. This is why they call the pineal gland chief of the soul because now this mind is seated in that part of the brain and the skull. And it is one that is trying to be universal in consciousness yet its been put down to one little body with one little person to do one little thing, to live a life.

But it's always tring to escape. And if for any reason that little worm like thing turns and can fall down within that saddle you die. That is clinnical death. What is clinical death? They say ceassation of brain wave activity or ceasing electromagnetic propogations of the spirit. You can get shot in the heart and you may or may not die. You may go into an immediate coma but you're not dead. As long as the EKG or celfudraft or something can pick up brain wave vibration and activity you are alive.

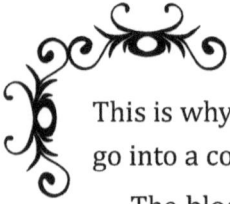

This is why the yogis can go starve themselves somewhat of oxygen and go into a comatic state and the blood, there is very little pulse to blood.

The blood doesn't seem to circulate but they are alive because their brain wave activity is still going on. Anything they can reconnect that brain wave with the body that brings a person back to life. This is why shock therapy can do it. Its much easier.Its an easier way of doing that, but that is metaphysical. When this is going on again this person now is honoring now what is called the worm turn. When the worm turns you die. Because it falls from the crossright position to a horizontal falls through the channel breaks that cord with the pineal and so it seams it didn't want to be here in the first place. Again that's why the pulsing at the top of the head, that's why the weakest spot is usually at the top of the cranial, that's why all that suturing and calcium deposit , now we drink a lot of cows milk and stuff and it makes it even stronger sutured and again that soul is now locked in.

The phrase the worm turns mean what? Pituitary twisting, falling, snaping a bridge with the pineal, the soul is free your dead your gone. So the phrase the worm turns is a little different from the worm in the corner. Again the metaphysical analyzation of the worm turns again and you have to make of it as you would. Another one of the things that is interesting too as they have gone into Egyptian and nubain archeological paleontological diggings to find supposedly what was part of the Nubian Egyptian society. They have come with certain symbols that have been used a lot. The symbol one is a circle which seems to be a cross beneath it. Which is also supposedly the sign for the female. But that circle cross has another name. It is called an unk. This unk the circle and then the cross is said to have been a metaphysical sysmbol. The other metaphysical sysmbol what is now used called the staff of life. You have heard the story of the old testament of Moses.

Moses had his staff and when he went before a pharoh he made the staff turn into a serpent and then the staff came back and the staff did a lot of magical things. They have even called it the magic wand and all

like this. Well these are very intersesting tales. But that's all that they are. The ceptor which is now called the staff was some kind of instrument with a round ball at the top and then like a cane sticking from it a point at the top and the bottom. You are going to have to use the power of the mind if you will, until I can make it clearer. The ceptor in most of your drawings and so when you went to tutunkhamens tomb or the Valley of the Kings, angra, or Luxor wherever you would they always showed the two together. And if you notice now the divine right of kings still has what, the kings crown with the crown jewels.

They have urasis that used to be that they had on tutuankhamen, akhnaten, rhamses all had these two snakes, they had the staff of life which is rulership that shows you were a king and they used to have some kind of ring or some kind of bowl that they put there that which was supposedly part of kingly authority. Well the unk was a type of instrument that had magical powers. The ring was a continious serpent. And then the four flanges coming from it. Each was made of a different material. I will not tell you how the material was made. But they are all bound within this little cross looking apparatus. And when you hold top energy would actually come out from your body if it could and then flashed down and it had to be grounded out. When this was pointed it was a weapon. When it was held it was resonant seeker. The divine right of kings also said that they all had the dividends rod by which you could find water. Well this was not only find water. It could attune to any element based on the amount of crystals and the amount of whatever you use within your unk. Your unk was a status of what your body could control. But when it called for certain forces due to the certain crystals that was in it, resonating with the crystal that is within your body which is where? In the head, in the pineal gland, you had to be grounded out and the ground out was your center. Which you can stick into the ground or rest on the ground or rest on an object to make contact.

The serpent at the top was what they call a magical, crystal now that the so call readers use. It was a round ball tuning to your frequency. It's

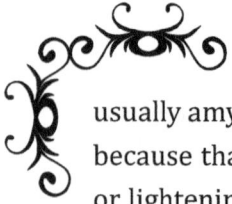

usually amythest or some kind of blood or something within that crystal because that's they way it had been grown. So this was your grounding or lightening rod. So any time you had the ceptor, you had the unk. And you would always see them standing in this position, they were ready now to do battle and to ground out to higher frequencies whatever you want to do. If you saw a person with an unk without a ceptor the person themselves had either grown to the understanding that he or she was already a lightening rod or they had lost it in battle.

Whichever it was because to use the unk without the ceptor was to make great promise with the body and chances. If you used the ceptor without the unk you actually ground out without no way to convey the power. So this unk and ceptor simply lets you understand again the forces of nature and the power of weapons that the ancients used. This thing could levitate things, with this they could set forth their own which is called ca. They could attract a ba. And of course the book that taught that all was the cabaallah. And of course now they have changed all of that to make you not understand where to look or how to look forward again. Unk and ceptor were interchangeable. Its like a white on rice. Without one the other didn't work. When you were you were a wizard, a wise person, you were a person who was anointed a Christos, you were one who understood the powers and how to harness the powers again. Everything that we have seen in the pyramid structure which by the way is not just in Egypt. There is no country on earth that does not have a pyramid somewhere on it. And at one time the entire earth was seemingly with pyramids and bringing it to being or helping it stay into being. All of these things still have latent power. The whole key on all of that was when human searches the stars for mankind. Man must go within to find God.

Because human and mankind are searching for God. Man is a fallen god trying to have and seek resurrection. All of these were parables but they had more truth in it than we seemingly understood. We are now begining to understand again the old teachings as they are brought back. There is talk about now what is called the swastika. We are told that

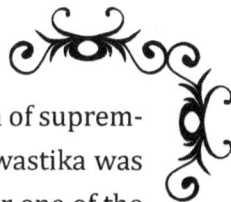

hittler and the third riech created the swastika as an emblem of suprem-
acy and to rule the world as they continue to say. But the swastika was
simply a take off on what is called the cross. If you remember one of the
other things that the ss used was the iron cross. It was a symbol of the
cross. And that is a takeoff also on the power of the unk, but on the cross
with directions. And the symbol that you see here is the same one on you
see on your seat, the iron cross or what is called the swastika. It is simply
a cross with direction. If you take a cross and you bring out the point
you will see again that it proves a good luck symbol on the cross symbol
if you would. It represents what is called the four great primary forces.
The four great primary forces. Which said that those four great primary
forces were fire, water, air, and earth which everything now on the earth
coporal physical life was made or could be taken from. In advancement
of physics it taught that this was not just a case that these represented
other forces and the best way without spending a lot of time to stay that
one represented what is called a static magnetic field. A second flange
of that is cross represented an electrostatic field. The third represented
an electromagnetic wave and the last one a resonating electromagnetic
wave or what is called a pulse wave. Until very recently it was said that
physical scientists here did not believe in a resonating electromagnetic wave and they were just beginning to look into an electromagnetic
wave they didn't believe in a pulse wave. Well as tesla showed as walkelly
showed as William right showed as Imhotep and so showed a pulse wave
is the frequency of everything.

It is the wave between electricity and magnetism. So, they may not
believe in it, but without it there would be no glue to the universe. That is
your pulse wave.emainating pulses coming form a mind and were living
in a mind field. Whenever you can harness this or get just a portion of it
you have some device that can take it all coalescent and then use it. Fire
water air and earth when look at the vibrations and the atoms of earth,
the vibrations in the atoms of the air, the vibrations in the atoms of water,
the vibrations in the the atoms of fire you will find them again.

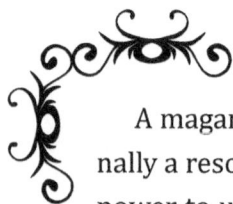

A maganetic field, a static field, an electromagnetic wave and then finally a resonating electromagnetic pulse wave. That symbol showed the power to unite all of these forces.And if you remember from one of the classes that we held or one of the lectures we held recently again and we were talking about the inner earth but also represented the cross or again the coming together of the els like frequency vents 90 degrees. Each one of those areas there is ninety degrees. And when you take all those ninety degrees and put them in a circle what do you have? Three hundred and sixty degrees of power, that's why they call it three hundred and sixty degrees of power. The unk represents the learning and understanding of three hundred and sixty degrees of power, plus an understanding of the four great primary forces. Once you have that and a ship, and a building,and a device you have universal power because you are harnessing it all and then putting it down so the grasper either in mind or in body can grasp an understanding and demonstrate the laws of the universe. Because it is that has said to be built. The human aura before were going to see if we can demonstrate how to see the human aura. It is the idea that around the body is a field of energy. Last week I demonstrated that field of energy. This week hopefully you will be able to see part of that field of energy.

If the field of energy is around the human body it simply means again that as your blood circulates and a your brain thinks it sends out energy. Energy can be manifested around the body and usually around the head first and it goes to all parts of your body. You know again what they call kinetic electricity. Ah you stand on a fur rug, you rub a cat or something, you touch a metal plate or you touch a light switch pie and you can hear. And if its enough discharge ut can even hurt and its been known to be able to harness it you had great power. I think there is,is there anybody here that hasn't happened to once in their life, somewhere along the line again. Well once you do that again you would have great power if you want. But it means you haven't controlled your field and something is pulling or making contact with your energy field. That whole idea is that

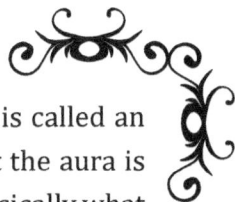

with an active brain and blood circulating you create what is called an electromagnetic field. An emf field. An emf is one thing. But the aura is not the emf. So please don't get it confused. That would be basically what you would first see when you start to tune into the aura. You will see that electromagnetic field, that static field of combines charges , it looks like a little light around the bottom.

The frequency of that of course can vary. But the aura is what the brain will generate as it changes its thoughts. The aura is to the electromagnetic field as a motion picture camera is to the screen that you are watching on TV. It gives it a field for it to play within in a confined space or else those energies would be dissipated. It closes the field and its within that electrical field that you generated which has a barrier, the thoughts can generate to that point and then as they crossover they die out. But while they are within that you can be trained to see those emanations. Closed in, best way again I can give you an analogy is that the aura is to the electromagnetic field as the screen again in a movie or the picture projector in a movie and camera is to the screen that it plays on. It gives it a point of recognition. A point where you can now see it. Other than that what happens? The projector screen if you have no screen up there it will go out to the wall and nobody will never see anything. Yet what was happening? It was still showing a movie from the projectors booth but you had nothing to play it on. So the playing on thing is your electromagnetic field. That's what all these thoughts.

The idea is that thoughts have frequencies. Remember last week we went to the sound of silence alright, some of you said you saw it and heard that. Those frequencies within you have power. And just as yiou began to tune into them inwardly you can see them on somebody else in training. And so the idea again the electromagenetic field is your screen set up by your brain and your blood. Your aura is now your thoughts being shown on the screen. So you can begin if you understand what the colors mean and what they do you can tell what a person's thinking somewhat, you can began to see where they are coming from. They

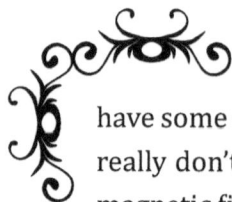

have some contraptions now that supposedly photograph the aura. They really don't photograph the aura but they is to photograph the electro-magnetic field in a way as the light bends again and it gives you a general idea of the thought resonances and the thoughts forms that are there. But thoughts are things, they have frequency, they have colors. Therfore anything with a color, anything with a frequency there are what you call twelve spectrum lights like our sun will have a color to it. Its just a matter then of trying to interpret the color as you see it on the screen. Once you began to understand how that works, you definitely must remember that the chakras are part of the same field continuum with the aura of energy.

If you go to any metaphysical seminar, any metaphysical class, or anybody who is into metaphysics, they all say we can read the and we know about chakras and all this kind of thing. Well maybe the you do. I still kind of like to teach it as I understand it and you find your truth about it as you would again. Chakras again mean wheels of life. Some refer to it as wheels of energy. It means that they are wheels because they always seem to be spinning. And if you slow down the vibrations you might only see a constant glow. But if you can speed it up they woud be spinning around like little wheels. Now they have said in many cas-es there are seven chakra centers. There can be 18 chakra centers. 13 on most individuals. But after the seventh one they are what they call beyond the body. Just like some saw me throw that little light out. You have contact with vast dimensions in space. But Seven is what most of the time you are taught. And seven is whats the most comprehensive one you can work with, the better. The idea is that each part of your body has energy obviously but that energy works with the glands and as the glands are functioning the glands throw off energy because the glands are supposed to be what?

The hormones through the blood circulation. All kinds of things work there, which meas that there is energy like a motor. If a motor is running and has an armature, it sets up a field.When your glands are working there is strong energy being manifested by these glands and you have seven basic ones again. You have what is called your sexual organs, you have what is called the spleen, or again later on if there call it the ovaries, you have again what is called the kidney section by the navel, you have what is called the heart area, you have what is called the throat if you would, youhave what is called the brow or the forehead where that little pituitary pineal is, and then you have what is called the crown. We kind of explained all of this in ourt classes today. Each of those is a set of organs and so.

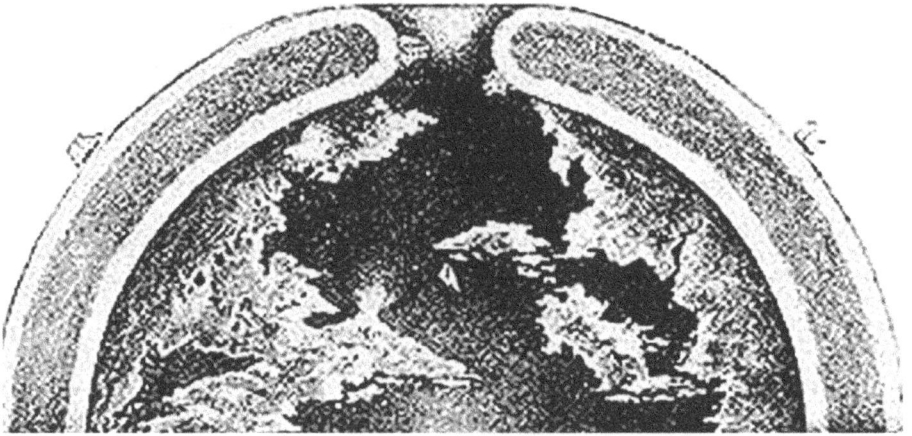

The World Within
Part 6-2

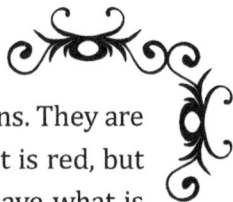

*I*f you have what thy called the root or the sexual organs. They are supposed to be a color within. Sometimes they say it is red, but there is a chakra center there nevertheless. If you have what is sometimes called the spleen, at one time under certain relious beliefs they didn't even teach you of the spleen chakra.Becuase they said it would cause you to be wayward. It would lower you down, because if you put too much concentration, since all the concentration was on the sexual organs anayway it would bring it too much. I teach the truth. I let you find the path between. The spleen would be another one. At the navel by your umbilical cord,where it is situated again there is said to be a strong energy field down there with a lot almost thinking capacity. What they call the lower brain. It encases the navel, umbilical cord. At the heart, the chakra center ther because the heart is a very integral portion. And if you notice in some metaphysical libraries the heart they will usually show with an eye, sometimes. Which means you see with your heart. To be able to see with your heart sopmetimes its better to be able to be seen with the eye.

Because sometimes they say the eye can be deceiving,but the heart always knows. Well I have found some emotional hearts but nevertheless whichever. At the throat of course is where you have the thyroid and parathyroid again and this is another functioning one. At the brow of course is where you have the pituary complex if you would and the pineal complex. And then at the top of course is where you have your crown shakra. Now they simply have different names for it. They call it the root, the spleen, the navel, the heart, the throat, the brow, and the top of the forehead the crown. Those are what they call the American or English names. Now a lot of this was said to have been derived from sandscript. Which meant that it was part of the druvidain techings that now equate that with Brahman Buddhitsic teachings saying that again they name it after the Indian. And were not talking about the Native American. The Indian east India or Indian people.

So you will find in some of the metaphysical literature and some of the metaphysical teachers that they will use names that were pronounced in

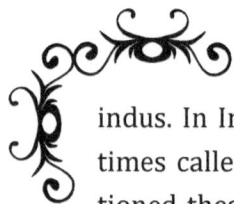

indus. In Indus valley in India again like that they have what is some-times called the root chakra which is just as good. I just simply men-tioned these names in case it comes up. Its called the mulancara hara chakra. That would be your root if you would. They have another that is called the swanashtara chakra which would be near the spleen or that combination in there. They have the monapura which would be in your pancreas and stomach area. The manupura chakra again. The throat would be called the veshutra chakra.The brow would be called the Isna. And at the top of the head thy have what is called the hastrara chakra or the crown. Now the other chakras again this is using the sandscriot terminology if you would.

Whether you call it the root, spleen, navel, heart, throat, brow, or crown, or you call it the mudahara, swanashtara, monaatah, veshuta, asnah, it doesn't matter its still the same concept. That at these centers are energy vortexes.Energy parts of power if you would. And that these things are always generating within the body. This is why they say its major organs there is energy and power. Sometimes you will find that hair will grow on some physical bodies at those major organs of power especially one that you use a lot. Because hair resembles a lot of energy going in and going out. And is also called the animal body to sometimes be effected again. Now what they call, no I don't want to go into that it makes it too techincal. Well in general what good are the chakra centers. Well its not about what good they are it's a matter if they exist.

These are wheels of light. They are always spinning and they have various colors. Understand I have never seen a chakra. When I was able to start to see chakras or when I was able to experience chakras that kept one color all the time. But they give this name because in most cases this is what you will first see if you could see a chakra. If you are looking at the root chakra or the madlahara chakra or the sexual organ it woud ususally be red. And usually very bright red like a fire or so if you would. Usually again at the spleen area what they call again the splenius plexuis again, it would be like an orange. And orange of course is made up of

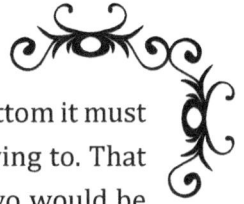

what two colors.?Red and yellow. Since you had red at the bottom it must be an orange or a yellow vibration somewhere you are moving to. That would be at the navel. And so that chakra inbetween the two would be a combination. So the navel there it would be what color? Yellow. When you go again sometimes in the heart they show it as green. But it will be a beautiful field green, an emerald green. Very glowing, very vivid green. When you go to the throat it would be a blue. Almost like it, it might be like, not that blue, but that blue you saw back there to the brighter blue that you pulled out. That would be again what would be at the throat. At the eyes and our brow it would be indigo. Kind of indigo looking if you would. And at the top of the head the swanashtara it would anywhere from a violet to a golden yellow. Golden yellow to violet again depending on how adavanced the thought, how much power you take in the center.

But this is what they call the basic colors of the chakra. The whole idea is that these things are always turning. They are always flickering. They are always moving. And even in the thoughts the Arabian nights used to call the book of a thousand and one dreams or the book of a million knights. These were all parables because its been said again what would be called the vashara crown the chakra it was always moving and peddled. So that the wheels were constanly changing a thousand and one different lights in the course of no time at all. Just spinning so fast that seemed to be the frequency and the rest of them would kind of slow down depending on the frequency and the power of the body that was possessing these kind of energy fields if you would.

So when you are using this kind of energy, when you are beginning to see the kind of things work. It means that all these are sources of power.To interrupt that power is to interrupt that chakra field. And therefore you are affecting that gland that organ whichever you are. If even in transferring colors what we call color therapy you can began to affect that gland, or that organ without ever doing anything physical to it, simply working with the power centers that is created, that is what is called the wheels of life. The wheels of life because they are always spinning

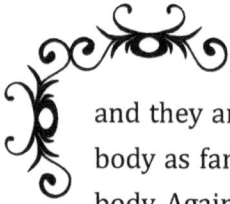

and they are always around the body. And how far they come from the body as far as the energy goes depends on the power generated in the body. Again. Its simply called chakras the whells of life.

The old parable in teaching simply said that original man was a spirit. And that the spirit had no physical qualities. It was simply light and energy. And as it condensed under a sun it beagn to then form the necessary organs and glands in a physical body. And those organs and glands still had contact with what was called the original person which was the spirit and the mind of that person thatthese wheels of life or what let you still connect with what is called the light body. Because when those wheels of life are turning through an advanced electromagnetic field you can actually create a body of a lighter texture or lighter elemental based on what the organ and so would be like if they were still physical but you could project them into space. That is what is called creating the light body. I think there is a person now talking about creating another kind of body. It's the same kind of way. It's using the chakras as power sources imagining them to be another type of condense light put your magnetic field and working with them. That's an advanced course in the whole thing of chakras.

The overview is that your organs give off energy. That your energy also creates organs or stabilizes them. Once the organs grow, once the organs are utilized there is still power there. If you were first a light body and energy created condensed organs, that's one way of looking at it. If you now have organs understand that they have power and they have energy and that energy can be fed upon, interfaced with, changed, whatever it would. That's the overall view of the chakra centers and probably one of the quickest classes and overviews of chakras that youll hear. But going along with all the other things that you have learned tonight maybe it will begin to make sense. Remember one thing, there is no truth until you decide what truth is. I only facilitate it by giving you an overview of the whole concept.

www.ingramcontent.com/pod-product-compliance
Lightning Source LLC
Chambersburg PA
CBHW021335090426
42742CB00008B/616